er

Modernizing Core Banking Systems

Deduction of a Technial Modernization Process for the Software Architecture of Core Banking Systems

Scholars' Press

Imprint

Any brand names and product names mentioned in this book are subject to trademark, brand or patent protection and are trademarks or registered trademarks of their respective holders. The use of brand names, product names, common names, trade names, product descriptions etc. even without a particular marking in this work is in no way to be construed to mean that such names may be regarded as unrestricted in respect of trademark and brand protection legislation and could thus be used by anyone.

Cover image: www.ingimage.com

Publisher:
Scholars' Press
is a trademark of
International Book Market Service Ltd., member of OmniScriptum Publishing Group
17 Meldrum Street, Beau Bassin 71504, Mauritius

Printed at: see last page
ISBN: 978-613-8-92787-7

"... Greed has poisoned men's souls, has barricaded the world with hate, has goose-stepped us into misery and bloodshed. We have developed speed, but we have shut ourselves in. Machinery that gives abundance has left us in want. Our knowledge has made us cynical. Our cleverness, hard and unkind. We think too much and feel too little. More than machinery we need humanity. More than cleverness we need kindness and gentleness. Without these qualities, life will be violent and all will be lost. ..."

Extract from The Great Dictator's Speech – Charlie Chaplin 1940

Abstract

In recent years the banking sector often faces the problem that outdated Core Banking Systems (CBS), which have their technological roots in the 1970s and 1980s, hamper their technological and strategic development, especially in connection with ongoing trends such as cloud banking, omnichannel banking, and the "Digital Bank". Due to constantly added extensions and modifications CBS often became grown monolithic systems, with a large degree of complexity and an extensive technology stack, which render their modernization a difficult and resource-intensive task. To help overcome these problems, this thesis defines Core Banking Systems formally and explores them from a scientific perspective. Furthermore, it develops a generic, architectural modernization process, which shall help banks and CBS vendors to transform their systems into an updated state of the art framework, which satisfies their current and future strategic requirements. The process is built in a cyclic way and contains eight sub steps, which form an individual modernization lifecycle for each functional module of a CBS. As a target architecture, the BIAN (banking industries architecture network) is utilized, whereas the developed process retains the flexibility to pursue other target architectures as well. This modernization process is particularly designed for the needs of Core Banking Systems and evaluated through the application of the process to an exemplary outdated CBS as well as through the qualitative review of experts in the field of CBS.

Keywords: *Core Banking System Modernization, Architectural Modernization, Modernization Process, Software Architectures, Software Evolution*

Contents

List of Illustrations

List of Tables

1 Introduction

1.1 Problem Statement

Today, there are different Core-Banking-Systems (CBS) on the market, which are fitted to the requirements of their customers. These customers are usually banks of various sizes, which either cover the entire field of banking in the broadest sense or which are focused on certain sub-branches of banking. The first commercial banking systems emerged with the digitization of the banking business in the 1970s and 1980s. At these times they were drafted and implemented with the technological and architectural means which were available then. Programming languages like COBOL, FORTRAN or IBM's RPG belong to these technologies. Furthermore, the interaction of these technologies were realized according to their technological characteristics.
With the introduction of newer technologies like the first version of C and C++, the implemented components and their functionality were kept as they were. New functionality was often added in newer languages with new functional aspects. This approach was continued for the following decades, with the effect that the technology stacks of certain core banking vendors became more and more extensive. In fact, this resulted in CBS vendors today, who offer Core-Banking-Solutions which still contain components based on technologies of the 1970s [84, 93]. As these vendors are usually profit-oriented and are also subject to commercial competition, they mainly spend their financial- and workforce resources in the implementation of functional added value, in accordance with the requirements of their customers. On the one hand, this is done in order to satisfy customer demands and on the other hand their intention is to remain competitively advanced in comparison to their direct business rivals. Correspondingly they spend little effort in the maintenance and continual modernization of their existing source code and the underlying architecture. Instead, components that have become technologically and conceptually outdated are wrapped in newer technologies and remain untouched for years according to the slogan "never touch a running system". However, the long term problem emerging from this situation is a decreasing maintainability of the old components, which is especially emphasized by the natural reduction of experts in these fields through retirement and staff fluctuations. Besides that, although CBS exist since decades they are scientifically a rather unexplored field, as they are very diverse in their functionality and mainly industry-related.

To overcome these problems, it is necessary to investigate CBS scientifically and to outline a formal definition of the term "Core-Banking-System". This consists of a description what a CBS is, what its purpose is and which functionality it should generally contain. Furthermore, it is also necessary to develop a process concept for the architectural modernization of CBS. The process concept will offer CBS vendors a roadmap, which enables them to modernize their CBS with a low amount of financial and human resources. In order to handle these requirements, this thesis will be focused on the two following scientific questions:

1. What is a Core-Banking-System, what is its functionality and what is its aim?
2. How could an admissible technical process concept for the modernization of a core banking system look like?

Based on these two scientific issues, this thesis is set in the scientific field of software engineering with a special focus on software architectures, and software modernization within the context of core-banking-systems in their entire functionality.

1.2 Motivation

The motivation behind this work lays in the business environment to which CBS are exposed. A CBS is a product that is mainly used in banks [53, 54], specialized credit institutions and in parts in insurance companies. These companies are subject to the regulatory measures of their respective financial market authorities. Both they and their governments issue regularly issue new laws which are to be obeyed by the credit institutions, as they would otherwise run into the danger of legal actions against them and possibly losing their banking license in the end. As CBS belong to the core IT-based tools for credit institutions to handle their daily processes, it is of crucial importance for CBS vendors to provide products, which fulfill the legal banking requirements of the respective countries. Especially after the financial crisis from 2007, which was to a big extent triggered by the banking sector, legal authorities strongly increased their surveillance of the financial market, which in turn meant that the number of new regulatory requirements increased respectively [35]. Consequently, CBS vendors are obliged to change their products more often in addition to the usual functional requirements which are demanded by their customers. That implies in turn that CBS and their architectures need to be more flexible to changes [55]. In order to gain more flexibility, CBS components need to increase their maintainability, scalability and technological independence. Hence it is of strategical importance for architecturally and technologically outdated CBS to modernize their software in order to remain competitive on the market in the longer term. A common problem during the modernization of a software component is the extensive amount of time-, personal- and financial resources that need to be invested initially. This is also a reason why CBS vendors avoided modernization attempts of existing functionality but rather invested into the creation of added abilities for the customer. However, the modernization of software components as well as the architecture reduces maintainability costs in the longer term and decreases the costs which are necessary to adapt existing functionality to new requirements. Another advantage of a consistent modernization process is the definition of a common product target software architecture, which defines a consistent technological thread throughout the product. In addition, a consolidated modern architecture reduces the complexity of the CBS software framework as a whole and is a better technological starting point for new functionalities, which in turn yields a higher competitiveness to vendors.

1.3 Aim

The main goal of this work is the deduction of a technical modernization process, which shall serve as a high-level guideline to CBS vendors, how existing old functionalities and software architectures may be renewed to a modern architectural CBS standard. To achieve this goal, a foundation shall be described which contains a description of CBS as well as software architectures in general. Also, a theoretical overview of existing software architecture modernization processes as well as the banking industries architecture network (BIAN) as a state-of-the-art standard shall be given. The BIAN [88] is a worldwide industrial framework that seeks to reduce interoperability issues between banks through promoting a common service landscape.
On this theoretical basis, existing CBS shall be examined and evaluated in terms of their architecture, in order to outline the current status on the market, in the context of CBS architectures. Afterwards, the examined architectures shall be discussed and compared to each other in order to find out their architectural strengths and weaknesses. Finally, an exemplary software architecture shall be described, which shall serve as an example for a proposed technical modernization process. This process shall then be evaluated and critically reviewed as the main result of this thesis.

Another major aim that is intended to be achieved in the course of this work is the scientific exploration of CBS in general. Up to now, a core banking system is usually seen as a "software product", which is highly industry- and practice related. Hence, they are functionally a rather diverse product, as there exists no CBS which contains the same set of functions as another. From a scientific perspective, a CBS may also be seen as an information system in the context of a bank, which usually covers its core processes and transforms its key data. But nevertheless, with the ongoing digitization of the banking business, CBS further extend their (already crucial) importance within the banking system. This is, in turn, a profound justification to create a common description for the term "Core Banking System", which shall set it apart from other systems under the hypernym "Information System". To achieve this, a formal definition of CBS shall be attempted, which will subsequently be complemented with a characterization of its main submodules and their respective functionality. Furthermore, functions that are typically included in its subcomponents shall specifically be outlined.

1.4 Thesis Structure

The overall structure of this thesis is divided into seven main chapters, which cover the topics around modernizing CBS on an architectural level from different technical aspects. Chapters two, three and four, are the theoretical part of this thesis and address Core Banking Systems, software architectures, and modernization from different aspects. They are also the foundation for chapter five, which is the practical section and contains a self-developed modernization process that could be used as a blueprint for the modernization of CBS. The aforementioned process is then evaluated in chapter six followed by chapter seven where a summary of the derived results of this thesis and a brief outlook is presented.

Within the theoretical section, chapter two gives a short overview of the current advancements in terms of modernizing software architectures, information systems and in particular CBS. Chapter three delivers a theoretical basis for the subsequent content and focuses especially on the terms "Core Banking Systems" as well as "Software Architectures" from a general point of view. First, an endeavor to scientifically capture the term Core Banking System and then a formal definition for this term is attempted. This is especially important as Core Banking Systems are still hardly addressed from a scientific point of view, despite their growing importance in the banking industries. After their definition, chapter three outlines and describes the core functional components forming a CBS as a whole. These functional components are not always contained in every Core banking product, but they are the functionality which is frequently found within a CBS. Next, the term "software architectures" is described (not defined as there already exist several scientific definitions for that term) and the criteria that are considered to make good software architectures are discussed. Afterwards, the elements of a software architecture are explained using the example of the 4 + 1 model of views, containing a conceptual, module, process and physical view, which are then completed by scenarios. Within chapter three different architectural styles and principles, as well as patterns, are characterized in order to complete the theoretical basis from a general perspective. The knowledge base of chapter three is the foundation of chapter four which distinguishes the connection between the previous terms and addresses modernization in the context of Core Banking System architectures specifically. To begin with, this chapter first summarizes selected architectural modernization approaches. Next, the difference between architectural modernization and software modernization is highlighted as it is a crucial aspect of the modernization process. More specifically, the focus of this chapter is the Architecture Options Workshop [35], model driven software- and architecture modernization [45, 46] and architecture-centric software evolution [35, 47]. Next, the chapter addresses "Banking Industries Architecture Network" (BIAN) [95], which is a standard for the architecture of CBS and may be used as a target architecture for the suggested modernization process. Its features and general characteristics are outlined. Following this, chapter four evaluates the architectures of five existing CBS based on public sources. The selected CBS are very different in their characteristics and are in parts "grown systems" and in parts architecturally designed from scratch. The main findings of the evaluation will then be summarized within the lessons learned section of the chapter and the CBS architectures will be compared to each other. The final subsection of chapter four contains an exemplary but fictional architecture of a CBS, which is used as an example for the evaluation of the subsequent modernization process.

Chapter five is the core part of this thesis and uses the previously gathered knowledge to create an innovative and self-developed modernization process which shall outline a potential mechanism for the modernization of Core Banking Systems, independent of their size, as well as functional- or technical constraints. The process is tailored to the specifics of CBS and consists out of several sub-steps, which are in parts recurrent. Chapter six evaluates the modernization process, which in itself is a two-step process. First, the process will be applied to the exemplary CBS architecture which was described in chapter four. Within that application, a demonstration of how the process fits a CBS is given and its strengths and potential weak points will be discussed. Second, the process will be presented to a number of software architect experts who have expert knowledge in the field of CBS and rely on decades of practical experience. They will be asked for their opinion under the use of a qualitative survey. The results will then be summarized at the end of chapter six.

Lastly, chapter seven summarizes the results of the previous chapters and provides an outlook into the future.

2 State of the Art and Related Work

The architectural modernization of Core Banking Systems, is a field which is not generally new, but it has not yet been examined intensely from a scientific point of view. Hence, the scientific works, which directly address the modernization of software architectures, in the context and with the specifics of Core Banking Systems that exist, are very limited.

However, there is related scientific work which covers similar fields such as the modernization of software architectures [50] in general, the modernization of software, software evolution in general and also the modernization of Information Systems [51, 52] as a hypernym of the term Core Banking System. Nevertheless, despite the lack of scientific coverage, considerable effort from different CBS vendors can be seen as the modernization of their products becomes an increasingly pressing need over time. In that context, this problem is addressed in a different way by vendors as opposed to the scientific community in that they use a much more practically oriented approach.

In the area of software engineering different approaches exist for the development of general software architectures. In the recent twenty years, software architectures have been developed for distributed software architectures as well as cloud environments (Aksit [1], Gomaa [2] and Schmidt et al [3]). These approaches are also subject to changing environmental requirements which lead to the development of different architectural patterns, such as micro services as the successor or extension to service oriented architectures. They are also influenced by the growing demand for flexibility as well as interconnectivity between different systems. Furthermore, the ongoing digitization within the industries results in extending the scale of software systems and corporate IT-landscapes, which in turn implies a growing complexity. From the perspective of software development, architectures are also affected by development trends such as Open Source development, model driven development, new disruptive technologies and technological-schematic changes (e.g. the introduction of NoSQL).

Besides changing software architectural paradigms, information systems (Bernus et al [4], or Scheer [5], Moto-Oka [6]) are also a field which has gained more and more importance since these systems generally enhance the global trend to computerized data processing in different industries. They are the hypernym of core banking systems, and can be roughly defined as "... a group of components that interact to produce information" (Kroenke, 2013, Page 9) [7]. They outline systems, which are used to transform information in order to complete the business processes of an organization such as a company, a department or a public community. Information systems exist in different contexts, a few examples are; hospital information systems, marketing information systems and generic management information systems. Among others in the course of the ongoing digitization of companies, these systems begin to become an integral part of company's IT infrastructures and from a technical perspective, they often consist out of various hard- and software components which are only loosely coupled with each other. In general, there is scientific work available which focuses on information systems and dates back to as far as the 1980's like the article of Pawlak [8], who attempted to lay out the theoretical foundations of information systems in general. Books addressing information systems were also already issued at that time discussing formal principles of an IS (e.g. Wood-Harper et al [9]). Nevertheless since then, information systems have emerged in different variations and in different industry specific contexts. In relation to that, core banking systems play a pioneering role as they had already appeared in the late 1960s and early 1970s due to the need to automate basic banking routines. These routines were then extended over time and began to slowly develop into the modern core banking systems which are used today.

In terms of software modernization, which is beginning to become a widely existent need in connection with IS, there exist a number of scientific works, which are based on theoretical and practical foundations. Research and further development of these systems has become more common since the early 2000s, yet they are still in an early stage of development as industries often perceive them critical. Some of these approaches will be discussed in more detail in section 4.1.
A well cited example in that regard is the paper of Izquierdo and Molina [10]. They follow a model driven engineering approach for software modernization, which entails basically extracting meta models out of existing (legacy) code and pursuing an attempt to implement the abstracted functionality in a different programming language along with a different architecture. In addition to them also Hoorn et al [11] also presents a similar approach as a case study in a German software project, which was modernized in 2011.
Another source of information is the ModelCVS project, which had been conducted at the Vienna University of Technology in cooperation with the Johannes Kepler University in Linz [78]. This project also follows a model driven development approach and aims to ease software engineering through supporting a shift from code centric software engineering to model driven development. It delivered a proof of concept which was further elaborated through the founding of a company on the basis of that project. This company successfully modernizes old code components to newer ones through the use of a meta-model. Another modernization approach for software architectures is the aim42 framework [79], which is essentially a collection of practices and patterns enabling software evolution, migration and improvements. Besides to the previously mentioned sources there also exist micro service approaches in order to modernize legacy software. An example is the work of Knoche and Hasselbring [40] who present a modernization process, that decomposes existing applications into a micro service oriented structure. They outline their process through the help of a real life application from the 1970s, which is to be transformed exemplarily. Also

Mili et al [41] research in the direction of service oriented reengineering of legacy applications, but they stay on a higher level and discuss the general issues and research directions in connection to refactoring to a service oriented architecture.

In contrast to software modernization, architecture modernization is a rather theoretical field but nevertheless an important field of study since a software architecture always defines the target blueprint of the underlying software that must align to the defined architecture. In regard to this topic, a well-known method is the Object Management Group's (OMG) Architecture Driven Modernization approach (Newcomb [12]). It is relatively practically oriented and designed for software architects, which are in practice confronted with the task to modernize an existing software architecture. It is related to the OMG's MDA approach (see section 4.1.2) and concentrates on the modernization of legacy architectures, based on formal models. This is achieved by trying to gather architectural knowledge from existing systems and formalizing it into so called platform independent models (PIMs). They may then be transformed into a target model, representing the target architecture which is automatically tested against the initial one with the use of test models. By doing so this approach keeps its focus on the architecture of a system and therefore remains platform and technology independent from the underlying code implementation [13]. Also to be mentioned is the work of Jamshidi et al [42, 43], who research in the area of micro services and perform pattern based and especially multi cloud architecture migration, which is a highly decentralized architectural challenge. They rely on a catalogue of fine grained and service based cloud architecture migration patterns in order to transform existing legacy applications and to make them ready for cloud environments. A similar direction is followed by Pahl et al [44], who also performs software system migration to cloud native architectures. In his work, he observes four different case studies, which migrated their applications to software as a service solution in a cloud and also presents a modernization process to enable that migration.

Besides to software- and architecture modernization, also scientific research is conducted in the area of software evolution. Software evolution not only covers one modernization cycle but is rather a descriptive term for the combined maintenance-, functional and modernization efforts, which are done in the lifetime of a software. In that regard Plakidas et al [38, 39] performed a multi case study concerning software migration and architectural evolution. He derives an architectural knowledge model, which shall support various real life platform evolution scenarios. A rather interdisciplinary approach is outlined by Miller. In his article [92], he evaluates current literature in terms of software evolution and verifies their impact on software engineering as well as the connected technological evolution. In terms of software modernization as well as evolution, decision support for major architectural and technological adjudications is often essential. In that context, Brand [57] analyses how runtime data supports software evolution decisions. His study was created in order to verify previously made evolutional assumptions in the vicinity of SAP and he presents a knowledge based development cycle in order to drive evolutionary software adaptation.

When it comes to the modernization of core banking systems as a hyponym of IS, the number of scientific literature becomes considerably more scarce, especially as science is lagging behind the industries' advancements in that regard. From a practical perspective numerous vendors of Core Banking Systems already put effort in their products in order to keep them technologically up to date in order to remain competitive on the market. Parts of these efforts include utilizing different modernization techniques, ranging from automated development approaches to the manual re-implementation of code. These techniques are especially relevant for them as they often work with their products for decades and usually a CBS vendor can hardly afford to create a new architecturally refactored CBS from scratch every few years. Due to these reasons they partially use architecture modernization techniques, like model driven development. In this regard vendors like Avaloq [80], Finnova [81] or Temenos [82] are to be named especially since they mainly use layer oriented software architectures with a rather extensive stack of technologies. Others also modernize old components through buying parts from more modern vendors and integrating them into their products in order to replace the old component with minimum effort. Another method that is widely used is to constantly replace the systems in order to gain a more modern system as well as to increase system flexibility and interoperability.
Another practically oriented institution in the field of CBS modernization is the already mentioned BIAN. It is a consortium consisting out of CBS vendors and banks, that gather guidelines which support the creation of state of the art CBS architectures. Their proposed architecture paradigm are service oriented architectures. In addition to this they also cover processes as well as best practices in banking software. However, in terms of functional coverage they are only limited to the central components of a CBS, namely retail, private and core banking (see section 4.2).

Besides to practical modernization approaches, case studies exist which outline and discuss major software modernization projects in different branches, such as the book from Ulrich and Newcomb [14]. They try to summarize architecture driven modernization with modernization techniques, scenarios as well as roadmaps, and show proof of the techniques' effectiveness with ten case studies of major architecturally driven software modernization projects. They summarize the respective outcomes from each project and highlight the drawbacks as well as the important aspects and events in the course of each modernization. On top of that, they discuss the lessons learned after each case study and in the end, they present some very central and context independent principles, which are a profound basis for future modernization and transformation projects. All in all, they gather an invaluable pool of experience in terms of architectural modernization projects in one book.

From a scientific perspective there exist a number of works which cover the modernization of parts of Core Banking Systems. For instance, Zimmermann et al [25] concentrates on the use of web service oriented software architectures as a part of a banking information system. Baskerville et al [16] describe the strategic value of service oriented architectures in the context of banking and in terms of flexibility as well as rapid changeability, although it should be noted that he does not follow a technical approach but more an economic one.

One of the few scientific works which directly address the modernization of Core Banking Systems from a technical aspect is the article from Kilimnik and Pavlovski [17], who discuss the transformation of Core Banking from a strategic point of view. To be more specific, they present their own experiences in that field and discuss different rollout strategies in order to successfully transform a Core Banking framework. They argue that using a Big Bang strategy, where an entire Core Banking Solution is replaced by another in one big release was implemented by some banking institutes in the 1980's and 1990's but is in general a high risk operation which is not recommended for use on today's CBS, as the scope, functionality and complexity of CBS has slightly increased since that time. As an alternative, they examine a phased deployment strategy where several pilot releases are taken into production mode, before committing a full go-live. Subsequently, they discuss a rollout strategy, based on the financial product, customer segment, region or the branch. These approaches usually face the challenge that they do not reflect the functional organization of the underlying Core Banking System and force either the customer group or the employees as a user group to use both, the old and the transformed system simultaneously throughout the duration of the migration. A solution to this problem would be to re-engineer the accessing clients of these user groups in order to abstract them from the functional split on the application side. Another approach is to roll out a transformed CBS in parts according to system- or functional domains, while the underlying database reflects the ongoing changes respectively. In the end, the choice of the implementing technologies and their supportability as well as the addressing of business risks are critical factors in terms of CBS modernization.

Another article, which directly addresses CBS in connection with modernization is Liu et. al.'s "SOA approach for the Progressive Core Banking Renovation" [18]. They state, that a progressive renovation of a core banking system is less intrusive and risky then a total replacement. Hence, they discuss a methodology to transform an existing CBS step by step into a service oriented architecture (SOA) based system founded on the concepts of business entities.

The methodology they use has a focus on a well-defined scope of applications which are to be modernized as a CBS is usually a large set of applications and components. Furthermore, they also focus on accelerated development in order to be able to react faster on changes and on component based design with the purpose to support an accurate functional granularity, integrability and reusability. In the first stage their method "component business modeling" (CBM) is carried out, where they map the business along business competencies and accountability levels. Through doing so, a bank is able to link its application landscape with business components, which in turn depict a direct mapping between its business and its applications. Next, the interactions between the defined components are captured which usually become the target entity bundles that are the basis for new applications. In the next step each target component is analyzed and the business activities which are conducted within its scope are captured in the form of defined business processes, which need to be aligned to the bank's requirements. After the business processes are created within the business components, each process is again analyzed in order to derive the involved entities. Following this they are then transformed into a solution model, which should contain a set of interacting entities. Finally, these entities are transformed into a service architecture consisting of data services and state transition services. In that regard a data service contains the querying and updating logic for a specific entity and a state transformation service encompasses the code to transform an entity according to its lifecycle.

In the course of modernization, the newly defined services need to be integrated with the legacy functionality as the business components are only replaced progressively. But in turn they can then be integrated to the life system during runtime. A problem that exists with this technique is the configurability of the services, but Liu et. al. resolve it by externalizing business rules (bank specific functional rules) into services again. The main advantage of this approach is, that banking specifics are separated from the core logic which in turn increases the adaptability and configurability of the resulting target architecture.

Like the previous works, Hussain et. al. [19] also examine Core banking systems from an architectural point of view, however rather than in the context of modernization they tackle this issue in a fundamental way. They propose a meta architecture for service oriented e-banking applications. Support and proof of the effectiveness of their proposal comes from the classification of e-banking use cases into inter-branch, inter-bank and middleware applications, with their own architecture but with the meta architecture as a common blueprint over the entire framework. The meta architecture in that context is a set of rules, guidelines and principles which governs the underlying architectures and hence increases the integrity and structure of the overall system.

3 Foundations

3.1 Core Banking Systems

This section outlines the definition of Core Banking Systems and briefly describes their historical evolution since the 1960s. Sub sequentially it describes the main modules of a CBS. In this context, CBS are in general very diverse in terms of their functionality, however the components described here are their functional intersection, which occur in almost all CBS.

3.1.1 Definition

Theoretically the term "Core Banking System" outlines a very specific area within the IT landscape of banks. According to Gartner a CBS is "... the back-end data processing application for processing all transactions that have occurred during the day and posting updated data on account balances to the mainframe. Core banking systems typically include deposit account and CD account processing, loan and credit processing, interfaces to the general ledger and reporting tools" (Gartner 2019) [83]. In other words a CBS is the application which technically covers the main use cases of a bank, namely the maintenance of current accounts, fixed deposit accounts, instant access savings accounts, savings accounts, loans and the management of customer's core data.

In practice the term is often used for a much broader area, as a CBS is usually combined with further application components, which depend on the type and business focus of the consumer bank. These components belong to banking functionalities like electronic funds transfer (in all retail banks), stock trading (in private and investment banks) and other functionalities which are related to the general information systems services like reporting, customer management, document management et cetera.

In general, a CBS as a framework is an information system which is situated within the subject-specific context of core banking. Information systems in turn are software systems, which allow users to transform business information within defined business processes. In the case of CBS the business information is on the one hand account data and on the other hand customer's core data, which are regularly transformed through the use of core banking business processes. In this regard, the central purpose of a CBS is to provide the bank clerk the right information at the right time, according to business needs. Additional aims of these systems include [66]:

1. To enhance banks efficiency through supporting the bank's personnel in their daily core business processes.
2. To automatically update customer accounts in regular time intervals.

3. To help banks to keep compliant with legal requirements, provided by the national laws and financial market authorities.

3.1.2 Historical Development

The first rudimentary CBS emerged with the introduction of computer technology into the banking industry in the 1960s and 1970s. Whereas the first aim was to share and increase the speed of information exchange between the branches of a credit institute. In the early years of CBS, each bank branch used to have a local server which contained customer data, as well as account data. The servers were offline and therefore disconnected from each other and information was exchanged at the end of each business day in the form of batches, which were processed by each server in order to synchronize its own data with the information of other bank branches. At these times the first CBS vendor companies were also founded, which often emerged from in-house CB solutions of bigger banks or were created as a joint venture business by several banks in order to satisfy their need for an electronically driven banking system. In 1981 the term "bank automation" [84] arose from the idea to automate banks' back office processes with the intention to centralize data operations as well as to increase their speed and cost efficiency. CBS solutions at that times often consisted out of a mainframe server which hosted the CBS application, the bank's CB data and a number of terminals which were dispersed over the bank's various branches. A prominent example are the main frame computers of IBM (e.g. Sys-tem/32 in the 1970s and AS 400 in the late 1980s) which were programmed with IBM's multi-paradigmatic RPG language. Their purpose was on the one hand to cope with the increasing amount of processed data and on the other hand to support new banking transaction mechanisms (like SWIFT) which were also introduced in the course of the ongoing digitization of the banking sector.

In the following years, CBS kept constantly growing in their functionality, according to the requirements of the finance- and banking sector. The commercial advent of networks and the internet which had become available to industries and home users impacted the technological aspects of CBS significantly, which in turn fueled the trend to conduct more banking transactions over electronic channels, now with a much higher speed than before. As a consequence, in the late 1990s banks began to offer Online Banking channels as a feature of CBS to customers as a means of easily conducting their banking business from their homes. This trend amplified substantially after the turn of the millennium, leading CBS to be required to technologically support account operations as well as funds transactions in nearly real time and to secure the communication method accordingly. Also from the architectural aspect CBS were largely confronted with a inclination towards dispersed systems. This implied new server client architectures, with various clients, depending on the user group (bank clerk, or bank customer) and their needs. Moreover, progressively more flexible and hybrid systems are currently beginning to influence CBS with emerging trends like Cloud Banking, Mobile Banking and integrated systems [93].

3.1.3 Modernization Challenges

Today numerous CBS vendors exist that offer various products containing different functionalities. The main challenge among them is that their products differ from each other to a great degree, which implies a wide range of heterogeneity and complexity in the field of CBS. However, the CBS is usually the core application within a bank's IT infrastructure, and is surrounded by many other applications. A large stake of the CBS are so called "grown" systems, which means that they were initially developed years or possibly decades ago and have afterwards been steadily extended with additional modules and functionality. Hence, CBS often grew in their original architecture which resulted in them being rather inflexible and hard to extend or replace due to their increasing complexity which had emerged over the years. Another problem is, that CBS are subject to ever faster changing functional and legal requirements which need to be obeyed. These requirements origin on the one hand from bank supervision authorities and on the other hand from the banking business itself, which is confronted with the constant need to change bank's strategies in order to keep in pace with ongoing changes in the economy as well as the society. Consequently, banks require more flexibility from their CBS in order to fulfil requirements but are impeded by CBS whose core components are outdated and are increasingly incapable to react to changing requirements. This increasing incapability is emerging due to technological constraints and the age-related reduction of software engineering staff who know, how to support these technologies. In addition, due to their monolithic character, the core components of CBS often contain strongly interwoven functional components, which are hard to separate from each other and therefore form large inflexible blocks.

Furthermore, seen from a CBS vendor perspective, each bank has different requirements to a CBS, which implies that a CBS vendor must have the technical flexibility to react to the diverging requirements of its customer bank. For instance, many CBS are developed for the regional bank market which is located in the national and international vicinity of CBS vendors. Consequently, they are customized towards the requirements of that market and there exist only few global solutions which are flexible enough to be deployed in any bank throughout the world. For instance, many CBS vendors focus on smaller banks and are neither capable of supporting multiple languages nor are they multi-tenant capable not to mention that they often support only one currency for account keeping. They begin to become especially unfitting for current trends which now include clouds, software- and service outsourcing, micro services or omni-channel ability.

In general CBS are subject to several factors which depend on the consumer bank and its environment, a few specific aspects for these factors include [67]:

- The quantity of customers in terms of the number of branches, the amount of its accounts and transactions and the overall volume of assets and liabilities that must be supported. The size of a bank is determined in the form of Tiers [85] which range from Tier 1 (approximately the 25 largest banks worldwide with millions of transactions per day) to Tier 4 (smaller regional banking institutes with usually less than ten subsidiaries).

- The application field, which depends on the organizational structure of the bank, the number of branches and whether the bank is operating on national or international level.
- The business scope of the bank, which entails retail, private, corporate, investment or transaction banking or asset management.
- The operational model, which may be either owner-operated or outsourced to data centers, co-sourced in connection with other banks or consumed from an application service provider.
- The deployment environment which influences the functionality of a CBS, like the language, monetary currency and legal constraints.

3.1.4 Functionality

All in all, due to the heterogeneity of CBS the functionality of a CBS can be summarized to the following five portions, which are at least partially available in the majority of CBS [67]. Aside the aforementioned aspects, the supporting functionality is also of vast importance. This includes attributes such as a workflow engine, which allows banks to individually adapt CBS according to their needs. This enables them to reuse existing functionality in order to create their own specific processes, which can then be used to transform their business data as necessary.

3.1.4.1 Management of Customer core data

This module comprises all functionality related to the core data of bank's customers and their relation to the bank. Customers can be roughly classified into two groups; private and business. Furthermore, they can also be divided into mandates or co-mandates of a bank account. In addition, a person can also be a direct and an indirect customer of a bank (e.g. if a person signs a guarantee for a debtor who owns a loan to a bank). In order to be able to manage customers, banks usually keep records of customers' stem data, relevant address- and contact data, as well as possible communication channels. Another important attribute of a customer's information is credit rating data which is necessary to assess the customer's financial situation which is a major part of a CBS customer core data component. To be more exact, the customer record contains data which can be separated into four aspects [68]:

1. Customer stem-, address and communication data:

   The central part of customer data is its stem data, like first- and last name. Former names, gender and birth date are also of relevance for a bank. Furthermore, banks often require additional customer data which are primarily used to estimate the customer's personal background and subsequently his solvency. This data may consist of whether the cus-

tomer is married, possesses academic titles or whether he has children. Also any migration background and his country of origin are often points of interest for a bank. In order to be able to identify a customer at the bank counter, banks keep a copy of a public documents for example a passport or a driving license. It should be brought to attention that these documents are also digitally stored as a part of the customer's core data.
For communication and legal purposes banks also keep record of the customer's primary postal address as well as any secondary addresses (in case the primary contact address differs from his registered address). Other uses for this information include being used to send bank statements as well as legal notifications. Additionally, the customer core data also contains metadata regarding the designation details (like "Mr." or "Mrs.") and also the manner which the customer would prefer to be contacted. Further communication data that banks store consist of (but are not limited to) E-Mail addresses, phone numbers and even Internet addresses. Customer core data does not only comprise personal information about the customer but also bank internal information which is related to the customer. For instance, banks store which bank lawyer is assigned to a customer in case of legal actions and whether a customer is a persona non grata or not.

2. Data regarding the financial situation of the customer:
   Data belonging to this section becomes especially important in relation to loans and situations, where a bank acts as a creditor for a customer. Hence, information like the monthly or annual income as well as the employer of a customer are of importance for a bank. Furthermore, information about account data, any loans, savings and properties which are related to the customer are also stored. Tax and legal information is also stored here as they may affect the liability of a customer. E.g. in case a company customer took a loan from a bank, key financial indicators of the customer are kept, like the ratio of equity in relation to debt capital or the customer's balance. Nonfinancial data is also stored in this branch, which is used to create a scoring estimation over the solvency of a customer. This scoring value is usually the result of a complex risk assessment, where data such as age, health, the kind of job, the gender, marital status, the duration of employment as well as the housing status are input factors. Also internal data which is collected from external credit agencies is usually recorded here.

3. Legal data related to the customer:
   Legal data in this context usually refers to the legal details of a customer or company and tax related data for customers. The legal form of a customer company is usually of interest for banks, as well as the main seat and the branch itself. Furthermore, information involving countries in which a customer pays taxes and whether they are subject to double taxation is of importance to a bank.

4. Product data:
   This module contains all connections of customers to a bank's products and services. This means banks keep a record of the bank accounts over which a customer is the main disposer or a co-disposer in connection with other customers. Also information regarding individual account conditions are stored here (e.g. debit and credit interests), which bank products and services a customer uses and also authorizations as well as warranties for other customers.

On the basis of customer's core data, banks create further administrative breakdowns which help bank staff to maintain customers. Typical functionality in this context comprises a depiction of the overall engagement between a customer and the bank. Also classifications of account managers which are assigned to a customer, as well as to sales branches belong to this section. Other tasks performed in this subdivision include reports which are generated on the basis of customer data, which cover various aspects of interest like customer ratings or customer related specifics like blocking notes and escrow settlements.
The management and maintenance of customer data is one of the corner stones of CBS. This signifies that a CBS should not only demonstrate the ability to show customers' stem data as well as respective metadata but also routines, which are necessary to create and update customer data. However, CBS usually do not delete data, but rather deactivate unused data records in order to be accessible for evidence purposes in the future. Hence, CBS usually don't contain functionalities to hard delete data. Another aspect which engages the customer's stem data is the ability to parameterize and customize the data and its metadata, as consumer banks may wish to change the underlying data model over time.

3.1.4.2 Electronic funds transfer (EFT)

The electronic funds transfer of a CBS covers all functionality, and as such covers the transaction of financial funds from or to an account, either within a bank institute or from one bank to another bank. In this context a CBS has to be capable to support all kinds of standard transactions from a bank account to another account, as well as debit payments, standing orders and their respective reverse transactions in case of an error or a cancellation. Also the processing of transactions in terms of dispositions, the consideration of account related limits and turnovers fall into the field of EFT. From this information we can gather that the electronic funds transfer service is not only responsible for the immediate electronic transaction of money from a sender to a receiver but also for the maintenance that follows a transfer. Like transactions from bank to bank (external transactions) EFT also covers bank internal transactions from journal accounts (inventory accounts) to sub ledger accounts (giro- and savings accounts). Within a CBS, transactions are usually done within so called Primanotas. A Primanota can be considered as stack of internal transactions

which are executed sequentially. A Primanota has both a creation as well as a conclusion record, which contains the lump sum of all debit and credit values of the transactions within the Primanota. The maintenance (initiation, adjustment and the closure) of a Primanota is a service which belongs to the functionality of EFT. In the context of interbank transactions on national and international level, EFT has to support a wide range of different kinds of businesses. Standard transaction interfaces such as via Swift or EAF/RTGS+, cheques, letters of credits, euronote facilities, foreign credits, guarantees, forfaiting and foreign currency accounts are instruments of respective transaction methods used by businesses which are covered by EFT.
The main characteristic of EFT is, that money is transferred on an electronic basis, without direct intervention of a bank operative. Seen from a bank specific aspect EFT covers several sub branches which will be briefly described in below [69]:

1. Cardholder initiated transactions: Dealings of this kind are carried out through the use of a payment card like a credit-, debit or an ATM card. These cards are electronically linked to a cardholder's bank account. Debit cards can either be topped up with a sum of money that is directly stored on the card itself and deducted with each payment, or in case of an ATM card, it is linked to the cardholder's bank account and the money is directly withdrawn from the bank account as soon as the cardholder uses the card to make purchases or to withdraw cash through an ATM. A credit card on the other hand is based on a revolving credit, which is issued to the card-holder by a card issuer. This credit usually has a limit and the customer can "borrow" money from the issuer in advance through the use of the credit card. After a certain period (e.g. monthly or quarterly) the issuer bills the borrowed amount of money to the cardholder and withdraws it from their bank account.

2. Direct deposit payments: A direct deposit payment is the immediate payment of money from a payer's account to the account of a recipient. Nowadays they are usually done electronically via means of EFT (either through online, mobile or telephone banking) but theoretically they could still be done through physically transferring cash from one bank account to another one. Direct deposit payments are commonly performed when one party wishes to pay money to another party, for example companies paying wages to their employees, or customers paying bills in exchange for a certain service. In the context of EFT a direct deposit payment consists of the amount of transferred currency in the target account as well as the account number of the source account accompanied by a valuta date. The valuta date marks the point of time when the money was effectively transferred to the target account and is therefore effective to the target account's interest calculations.

Aside from that the name of the source account owner and a meaningful field of information (payment reference) is typically specified in a transfer in order to enable the recipient account owner to recognise from whom the payment is from [70].

3. Direct debit payments: Transactions where the receiver sends a request to the bank to directly deduct money from a payer's account are generally referred to as direct debit payments. In order for the payment to be deployed successfully, the payer must authorize the recipient to deduct money in advance by notifying their bank. As an example, in Europe the majority of payments are conducted using the SEPA procedure (Single Europe Payments Area). In this method the payer issues a SEPA mandate to the receiver, which authorizes the recipient in both his as well as the payer's bank to deduct money on a recurring basis from the payer's account as long as the mandate is not recalled. Furthermore, the payer's bank may cancel direct debit payments if required, for instance if the deduction breaches the payer's account limits. In general, direct debit payments are mainly used to automatically pay recurring bills which are issued by corporations to private customers (e.g. monthly bills of an internet service provider or a provider company to its customers). However, the boundary of direct debit payment only covers the authorization and the mechanism of payments from a payer to the recipient. The circumstances in which the payments take place (frequency, amount, regularity and deduction date) are usually subject to an agreement between the payer and the receiver and not influenced by the executing banks [71].

4. International wire transfers: International wire transfers encompass international money transactions, including currency exchange from a domestic currency to a foreign currency through an international banking network. They are usually the cheapest and one of the fastest ways to transfer money between accounts, regardless of currency or the location of the receiving bank. In order to conduct a wire transfer, a customer requests their bank to send a specified amount of money to a target account of another bank. The recipient account is identified through a worldwide unique IBAN (International Bank Account Number) code and the receiving bank through its corresponding BIC (Business Identifier Code). Next, the bank uses a secure banking network (such as SWIFT, CHIPS or Fed-Wire) through which it submits a message to the receiver bank. The message contains the payment details as well as its settlement instructions, like the valuta, and is effectively a request to transfer the specified sum to the recipient. As soon as the message is received by the receiving bank, it transfers the amount from its own monetary base. In the background, it accounts the amount to the issuing bank via reciprocal Nostro and Vostro ac-

counts. The balance via reciprocal accounts may also include recipients that are intermediate banks since in some cases the receiving bank does not have a direct corresponding relation to the sender's bank. Usually the sending bank as well as the receiving bank and intermediate institutions deduct fees from the transferred amount of money, therefore the receiver will always receive less money than the sender transmitted.
SWIFT (Society for Worldwide Interbank Financial Telecommunication) is the main international banking network. Its focus lies on providing a standardized, secure and reliable environment for banks in order to communicate with each other. However, as mentioned before, SWIFT itself does not transfer real funds but rather sends payment requests in connection with settlement instructions. These inquiries are to be settled between two corresponding banks and are technologically transmitted via an IP network infrastructure. The SWIFT technology is considered unaccountable for the messages which are transferred as well as the participating banking corporations. On the other hand it is responsible for providing both the secured network as a usable infrastructure and a defined set of syntax standards for financial messages, based on XML. Additionally, SWIFT also makes the corresponding software available as well as further services which enable financial institutions to transfer payment messages across its network. Architecturally, SWIFT is based on a centralized store-and forward mechanism which allows this technology to guarantee the reliable transmission of a payment message through a high grade of redun dancy in terms of hardware, software and the participating personnel. Physically, SWIFT works through three data centres which are located in the US, the Netherlands and Switzerland and currently (effective 2019), it transmits around 32 million messages per day through its infrastructure [94].

5. Electronic bill payment: EBP is a feature that has been available to banking customers since the 1990s via telephone but has received more recognition with the emergence of online banking. EBP is essentially an agreement between the customer and their bank to pay bills that are issued to the customer on a predefined day each month automatically. The bank is capable of reimbursing the bills either via electronic payments or cheques, however the responsibility of ensuring that the balance of the paying account is sufficient falls to the customer. EBPs may also be accounted against credit accounts, where the customer is required to pay a certain interest rate for the account balance. In some cases, banks may surcharge transaction fees to bills, which are handled via EBP [72].

3.1.4.3 Account current

Account current is a major part of CBS, containing all functionality related to the maintenance of accounts. Theoretically, account current is a standard form of financial service processing between a creditor and a debtor which are in a constant business relation with each other. In the context of banking, each giro account is a special form of account current business on the basis of a giro account treaty, issued and signed by both parties during the creation of a giro account. During a bank's business day a giro account may be subject to credit postings and debit postings. These postings and their sums of currency are calculated to create a daily sum. The daily sum may be either positive or negative and is the basis for the calculation of interest rates for the account. The interest rates as well as further fees are then calculated in the course of recurring account closings. Generally, banks have daily, monthly, quarterly, semi and annual account closings, where depending on the account type the final balances of their accounts are calculated. The structure of a bank account is usually organised into a journal, which contains all bank internal inventory accounts as well as a sub ledger containing all customer owned giro- and savings accounts. The calculation service of accounts' interest rates and balances in regular time intervals is one of the core functionalities of CBS. How interest rates are in fact calculated differs often from bank to bank and is also influenced by the account type and legal regulations accordingly [73].

In addition to the financial closing of internal- and customer accounts, the services of account current also include the maintenance of various account types and more specifically the parameters which are connected to a certain account (type). Accounts are typically sorted into the following categories; private, salary, various compensation accounts and foreign currency accounts, depending on whether the CBS supports account-processing in different currencies. All in all these accounts may be classified as either giro accounts or savings accounts, and depending on the product as well as the individual owner (and his solvency and significance for the bank) of each account different conditions take effect. The different kinds of conditions affect debit interest rates as well as credit interest rates, which are in connection with overdraft charge rates and in the case that an account exceeds its overdraft facility. These interest rates may occur in different forms such as graduate interest rates, variable or supplementary interest. Additionally, the account current has to contain maintenance functionality for account fees which arise due to the preservation of the account as well as additional services, which are billed to the account holder. Verification of limits is another of the typical functional aspect of the account current module. This feature comprises the regular validation of account operations (bookings) in accordance to any limits which shall not be exceeded. As a standard example, if a customer decides to issue a transaction which exceeds the overdraft capacity of his account, the transaction should not be executed but instead dropped.

Except from these conditions there exist many more parameters which are related to an account as a "consumer product". They are persevered in a non-productive model account, which serves as a preconfigured template for a newly created customer account. Hence, each account template represents a certain account product, which is in turn a part of a defined account family. Examples for such parameters include the scope of transactions that may be issued through the account. For instance, savings accounts may only allow transactions to a predefined reference giro account, while being able to receive credit postings from any other account. In turn, the reference giro account may be permitted to issue transactions to any other account. Account current does not only maintain these preferences for accounts throughout the process of their creation (which is based on model accounts), but also during their "productive" lifetime. Parameters may be modified in the course of their existence, either through adjustments of the account by the bank clerk according to changing circumstances, or through automatic processes of the CBS. These changes also need to be covered through account current and recorded internally for evidential reasons as well as legal requirements. Regular account statements are used to make alterations to the account transparent to the customer [73].

A rather specialized field of account current is the reform of the assignment of roles from account to customer or vice versa, and switching between customer and account, which may occur in the case that a customer company no longer exists (e.g. due to a merge with another company, or if the ownership is transferred to another party). In addition to product parameterization, account current also involves the maintenance of internal parameterization systems such as number systems, which are used as a reference for the creation of accounts, identification of transactions, or internal general ledger positions. Through the usage of number systems, data entities within the CBS can be uniquely identified and categorized into certain products (e.g. the IBAN of an account may already contain the information according to its numbering on whether the identified account is a giro or savings account).

Account current also contains information on which type of card is available to a certain account or customer. Furthermore, it contains the type of account, along with information about its functions. Usually the majority of parameters of accounts and cards are predefined by the bank or a third party which offers its card products via the bank. Card management from a technical perspective is a major component within a bank's infrastructure and entails the maintenance of cards as well as their related products, the termination of their validity on the closure of a customer accounts, and the management of card terminals, such as ATMs, payment terminals or self-service machines.

Another trait of account current is all functionality needed for direct cash operations at the bank's counter. Using this service, a customer may deduct or deposit cash from or into his account without a payment card but with an appropriate legitimation document (e.g. a passport) via a bank clerk. The capability to support transactions at the cash desk is also a part of account current, however, in the last decade, direct cash transactions in the bank were slowly replaced by more convenient channels like online banking. Accordingly, the number of electronic transactions increased, which resulted in a trend to assign selected parameterization functions to the customer via Online Banking. E.g. customers are given the freedom to change minor parameters related to their accounts such as the way account statements are issued, certain maintenance functions and the limits of their credit cards [73].

3.1.4.4 Trade and investment

Trade and investment covers all functionality of a Core Banking System related to money transactions, savings businesses as well as certificates, securities and treasures.

In terms of money transactions, a CBS has to be able to uphold all necessary conditions that are obligatory for a money transaction in order to be executed. These conditions take account of exchange rates, fees, and interest rates. Important changes in this details of a transaction are mainly in the dates on which a certain amount of money became effective on an account, prolongations, intermediate disbursements and capital changes in general. All of these details imply an effect on the amount of money that was available at a certain point of time on a certain account, and therefore has an effect on the calculation of its respective interest rates. For instance, if the balance of account A is increased due to a credit entry then this amount has to be considered in the calculation of credit interest rates at the next account closure, even if the same amount is deducted after one day. In case the balance of an account is reduced beyond zero then this has to be considered with a corresponding debit interest rate and moreover with an overdraft charge rate in the case that the account exceeds its limit. Through the use of their CBS, banks usually carry out the calculations of the sum of daily credit and debit postings (during the daily account closure) for every account. Their balance results in a daily sum, which basically shows how much money was available on a specific day on a certain account. This balance is used for customer visible account closures, like a (monthly) quarterly or annual closure. Furthermore, if the valuta of an amount is changed manually then the timespan on which it is available, is also changed. This in turn implies that the interest rates for a certain amount have to be corrected, even if the account was closed for the time period in which the valuta was effective.

In connection to savings business, a CBS needs to cover all aspects which relate to it including the maintenance of savings conditions, rates of interest, account closures and premature terminations. This functionality is already covered to a large extent with ordinary account keeping, as is described in the previous section. The only difference is that a customer pays a certain amount of money into a savings account and is not able to access the money for a certain period of time. In return they will gain interest rates for the deposited sum according to the agreed conditions. The maintenance of the previously mentioned conditions may be sustained through the use of model accounts, in a similar way to giro accounts. Account closure and the calculation of interest rates are usually done within a daily, monthly, quarterly or annual account settlement run. The only

exception is the premature termination of a savings accounts since this results in the CBS needing to be ready to calculate respective interest penalties.
Regarding savings certificates a CBS must be capable to support the maintenance of issued certificates from the bank and it must be able to calculate current interest rates, much alike a loan. Furthermore, certificates may also be annulled or compounded at some point in the future, as they might also need to be repaid to the customer, which means that a CBS also requires the functional ability to support this task. However, since bank certificates are a product which is not used very often, it is not seen as one of the central components of a CBS.
Much more important and often referred to as the main part of trading and investment banking is all functionality in connection with securities and treasury. Security trading contains all security products ranging from stocks, via funds and bonds to options, as well as futures and other derivatives. In this aspect, a CBS usually contains functions for the front office, such as portfolio analytics, where different kinds of stocks need to be shown. These visual services are associated with a depository of different views and dashboards and must also support risk management on them. Other front office functionalities are modelling as well as the risk simulation of securities before and after they are traded. The CBS also has to cover both legal as well as banks' internal limits in order to prevent illegal trading methods. In terms of risk management, stress tests, liquidity risk, market risk and credit risk are all components which are of vital importance. Aside from that, the Value at Risk and regulatory reporting to financial market authorities need to be functionally depicted in a CBS' trading module.
Another field in terms of trading is cross asset processing, which outlines that all kinds of assets should be handled over all stages of a trading transaction, from the placement of an order to its payment and its confirmation. This workflow should be supported by a CBS automatically in order to enable rule based automated trading. Investments also need to be documented from an accounting as well as reporting point of view. This documentation involves keeping the position of each transaction, treasury management, the preservation of the sub ledger as one of the central parts of a CBS and data quality management. Also fund administration, as well as the calculation of the Net Asset Value are capabilities which are expected to be supported by a CBS.

Treasury itself is largely integrated with trading but in contrast to trading with stocks, it consists of trade with currencies as such. In this context the management of foreign currencies in combination with their exchange rates to each other are an important functionality of CBS. Further tasks in this field include gathering the required data from a reliable source and updating changes within the CBS on a real time basis [74].

3.1.4.5 Loans

In addition to account current and customer data management, loan management belongs to the central components within CBS in general, as the issuing of loans is a vital part within the banking business. First of all, a CBS has to cover all required types of loans (at least the one which a customer bank intends to issue to its end customers), whereas private and business loans in all different variants are the most widely spread kinds of loans. Apart from that, also consortium loans, factoring and swaps play a role. And additionally to them the leasing business (e.g. of cars or expensive goods) is an increasingly developing sector within bank's loan branch. A CBS also has to support the lifecycle of a loan, which roughly covers the following steps:

1. Loan application: Consulting the customer which loan is suitable, based on their requirements and obtaining basic information from the client.
2. Loan processing:
    a. Obtaining rating data about the customer including his financial situation, risk factors, financial credibility, and potential collaterals.
    b. Reaching an agreement with the customer on the terms and conditions of a loan (runtime, interest rates, periods of payments, kind of loan, etc.).
    c. Setting up the loan as well as the loan contract.
3. Signing of the loan contract.
4. Loan contract closure:
    a. Opening a loan account and disbursing the funds.
    b. Closing the contract legally through an attorney (if necessary).
5. Serving and maintaining the loan:
    a. Monitoring the loan in terms of timely repayments, recurrent loan risk rating.
    b. Collecting recurrent interest (if they are not repaid at the loans maturity) as well as collecting potential service fees.
    c. Terminating the loan as soon as it is repaid.

Aside from the standard functionality within a loan's lifecycle, a CBS also needs to encompass special cases such as changes in the loan conditions during its term or the treatment of a loan in case the customer fails to repay it. A bank usually offers different loan variants in different conditions to its customers. Respectively the CBS needs to be able to support these conditions, which includes different methods of calculating interest, provisions, fees and it must be able to handle refinancing rates (in order to be able to issue loans, banks often refinance themselves on the interbank market). As soon as a customer requests a loan, a repayment schedule containing the expected interest rates over its runtime, based the offered conditions, is required. Hence a CBS needs to be able to calculate fees and interest fees to a loan, depending on given parameters like the runtime, the kind of credit (fixed or variable) and a given interest rate. In order to rate a customer's credibility, banks often analyse their payment conduct based on bank statements. Furthermore, they usually also reach out to credit agencies with the purpose of gathering external information about a customer's credibility. Additionally, they also take further factors into account such as a potential debtor's age, his income, his marital status as well as his overall financial situation (e.g. his monthly income in comparison to his monthly expenditures). For business customers the same process is carried out only based on financial core data. From that, information banks create a central customer rating which is in turn reflected in the conditions (risk surcharges) under which they offer a loan to a customer. They also recurrently rate ongoing loans based on the repaying mannerisms of a customer [73].

In addition to ratings, banks also need to maintain loans. In the case that a customer does not pay his rates in time, the bank needs to send dunning letters to him and react accordingly internally. Banks also supervise whether internal overdraft limits are exceeded and put selected loans on a so called watch list, in case their rating falls below a predefined threshold. Sometimes a customer may ask for a respite and if loan evasions occur, the bank needs to be ready to sue the customer and to initiate an absorption procedure enforced by the jurisdiction. In this situation, a loan is usually handed over to an internal workout department with the aim to minimize or prevent losses from a defaulted loan. Another vital part of loan management is the maintenance of collaterals which may have all forms of value ranging from art pieces, machines and real properties to financial stocks. A bank needs to be able to enforce the execution of securities in case a loan fails.

Finally, loans need to be covered from an accounting perspective. This means their settlements must be accounted and assessed, initial and termination bookings must be conducted and also certain special cases such as deferred interest, early redemptions and possible resulting prepayment penalties need to be covered from an accounting aspect. These accounts in turn need to be reflected in the end balances (monthly, quarterly, and annual) as they usually play a large role within the day to day business of a bank.

Accordingly, a CBS should contain the required functionality in order to allow banks to execute the above described tasks [73].

3.2 Software Architectures

From a general perspective software architectures are a generic field in the area of software engineering. Hence, in common literature they are defined and described in multiple ways. The following section outlines the main definitions and will also describe common elements and styles of software architectures.

3.2.1 Defining Software Architectures

Before entering the field of software architectures it is necessary to define the concept "Software Architecture", as the term refers to a vague field and is therefore often perceived differently in different contexts. A variety of definitions for the term software architecture exists, however the definition from the IEEE board in its Standard 1471-2000 seems to be the most reliable. It defines an architecture in a software intensive system as "the fundamental organization of a system embodied in its components, their relationships to each other and to the environment and the principles guiding its design and evolution" (Maier et al, 2000, Page 6) [20]. According to this standard, an architecture is a fundamental organization of a software system which describes its conceptual outline. From a professional viewpoint a software architecture can also be seen as a sub discipline within the field of software engineering, which covers the process of creating an important high level description of the underlying software project. The "description" of a software project is subject to external constraints (costs, time, complexity and technological restraints) which should be taken into account in a solution. Furthermore, an overview of the collaboration of the various components of a software project should be included. This will serve as a blueprint that is necessary in order to be able to understand the main objective of the project and to implement it according to a single consistent concept.

According to Dustdar et al [21], a software architecture can be on the one hand seen as an abstraction and on the other hand as a building plan of a software project. In terms of the abstraction, one of the main goals of a software architecture is the abstraction of technological aspects, which results in a reduction of complexity. The abstraction is conducted through the aggregation of details and the summarization of functionally similar elements to functional- or topological components. An abstraction of a conceptualized software should already take functional as well as non-functional requirements into account and should consider influences which have an impact on the development and the utilization of the software. Another goal of a software architecture is to make the software concept understandable and verifiable to all stakeholders that are involved in the development and the usage of a software. An advantage of the abstraction is its reusability in other software projects. This means that as a software architecture depicts an abstract model of a planned software product, it may be reused again in the same way or with adaptions in other software projects, which are in turn influenced by the standards, decisions and solutions which are contained in the software architecture.

Seen as a building plan, a software architecture describes the topological fractionation and the communication between the sub modules in a software project. Furthermore, it contains high level standards and characteristics that are to be obeyed during the implementation. The blueprint can be drawn in different levels of detail, which produces an overall structure of a consistent architectural concept of the project. The advantages of this approach are the different levels of detail and abstraction, as well as the fact that the architectures of external software components along with their interfaces can also be included into the software architecture blueprint. Another advantage is that a software architecture serves as a documentation of early design decisions, which emphasizes the influence of external constraints on the solution. Software architectures in general have to be disassociated from system architectures, as a software architecture in its classical perception is restricted to the architecture of a software itself but does not directly take the underlying hardware infrastructure or network into account. These details are conceptualized in a system architecture.

Software architectures can be separated into different categories depending on their scope. Architectures which are limited to a single software project are referred to as "standard" software architectures. In contrast to that, architectures which extend over a line of functionally similar software projects (product family) are named "product line" architectures. Moreover, software architectures which serve as a reference architecture for software products in a certain context (for instance a Core Banking System) are domain specific software architectures. A software architecture can be further abstracted to a domain independent abstraction level such as architectonical styles or patterns like the model–view–controller (MVC) model. They depict standard styles of implementations and are adaptable to all software projects. However details may vary depending on the project, its requirements and usage environment. Aside from the terms clarified above, architectures in the context of software may also exhibit different aspects which are tightly related to a software project. Information, processes, businesses, databases or other systems are instances which may also be considered in an architecture. Naturally, distinctive types of architectures exist for these separate systems as well, for example information architectures. Process architectures, database architectures or system architectures show the organization and collaboration of a system in terms of the given layer.

3.2.2 Quality Attributes of Software Architectures

After the definition of software architectures, it is necessary to outline the quality attributes of a software architecture. In general, software architectures cannot be directly valued as "good" or "bad", but they can be measured by the extent to which they fulfil their purpose. There also exist methodologies for the assessment of architectures and how well they fit the requirements of a certain software system as well as stakeholder conditions which are included in the development and the utilization of the resulting application. Examples include architectural trade off analysis methods [22], various (aspectual, scenario based) software architecture analysis methods [23, 24, 25] or certain review and evaluation methods [26, 27, 28]. In terms of overall software- and computer system quality there exist standards like the ISO/IEC 25010 norm [96], that defines a quality model which may be applied to computer systems. However, its scope concentrates on computer- and software systems from a holistic perspective and does not focus on software architectures.

In general, it is difficult to outline generic criteria which are applicable for all architectures as they are always dependent on specific requirements regarding the software quality, costs versus benefits, the functional requirements as well as environmental constraints of a project. However, Bass et al [56] defined several quality criteria in their book which are bound closely to software architectures. These factors encompass attributes such as performance, reliability, availability, security, modifiability, portability, functionality, variability, ability to be segregated and conceptual integrity. Of course this list of quality criteria has been revised as important factors like scalability and flexibility or technological independence have been adjoined, since these characteristics have become an vital aspect of architecture design. Nevertheless, the following guidelines have been defined for a "fitting" software architecture:

- The architecture of a software should be the product of a single architect or a small group of architects.
- The architecture should be subject to clearly formulated technological and qualitative requirements.
- The software architecture should be documented in a notation which is comprehendible by all stakeholders who should also be actively included throughout the design process.
- It should be meticulously analysed and verified against qualitative attributes.
- It should outline the base frame for the later implementation with consideration of the communication paths between compartments.
- The architecture should disclose resource constraints and demonstrate their solution.
- The architecture of a software system should be divided into functional modules, where each module contains a distinct amount of functionality and communicates with other modules through defined interfaces.
- The modules should be decoupled as loosely as possible in order to facilitate separated development and in order to keep the effects as local as possible, in case a module needs to be modified in the future.
- An architecture should never be dependent on a certain technology or a specific version of a product.
- The interaction patterns of an architecture should be minimal and simple. It should be ensured that the same mechanisms are always executed in the same way to ensure that there is no redundancy.

3.2.3 Elements of a Software Architecture

Software Architectures always depict a certain view on a software system [56, 57, 58], whereas a certain aspect is highlighted. Therefore, a number of views exist in the context of software architectures. In this context the 4+1 model of views is a comprehensive example.

3.2.3.1 The 4+1 Model of Views

After the basic definitions and quality requirements of software architectures were outlined in the preceding chapters, it is necessary to describe the main views of a software system, where each view can be seen as the abstraction of a software in connection to a certain aspect. In this regard, a view neglects architectonical information that is unimportant for the aspect, but highlights attributes according to certain criteria. Based on the IEEE 1471 Standard a view is defined as "a representation of a whole system from the perspective of a set of concerns" (Maier et al, 2000, Page 3) [29], however there exists a common approach which is based on five "views". The so called 4+1 view model, which was first described by Kruchten in 1995 [30]. It consists of a logical or conceptual view, a module or development view, a process view and a physical view which are then combined in scenarios. Illustration 1 shows an overview over the model and the next sections describe the views briefly.

Except from Kruchten's 4+1 model, also other software architecture view models exist, like the three-schema approach as well as extensions of Kruchten's model, however the 4+1 model has gained a distinct popularity in software projects [77].

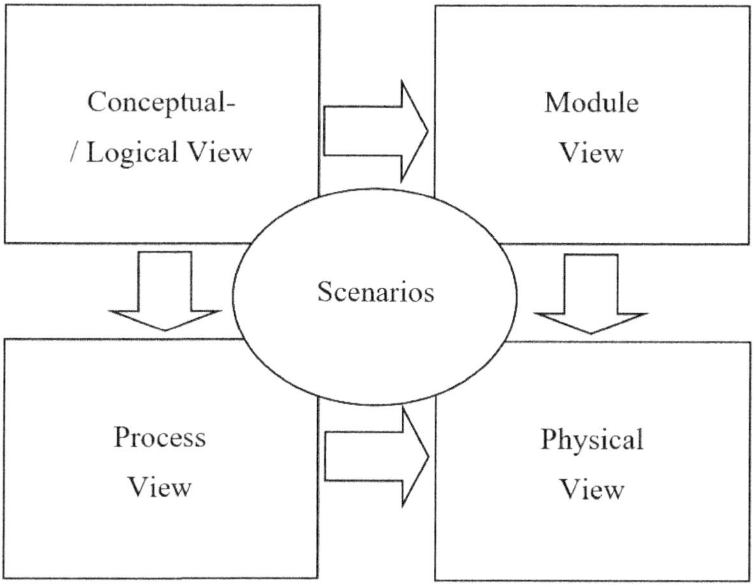

Illustration 1: The 4+1 Model of Views

3.2.3.1.1 Conceptual View

The conceptual view depicts the logistics of the system behaviour, which shall be implemented through the underlying software component. It is comprised of a view over the functional requirements and is usually the first architectural design response to the requirements of a customer or client [31, 41], as well as an analysis of the domain in which a software operates. It displays the central entities of the given domain as well as their interactions and connections with each other.

Usually the conceptual view is drawn with the use of a graphical notation which is capable of describing conceptual or logical designs through entities and relations or connections, like UML diagrams. However, the conceptual view of a software architecture is not a static design process which is done once, but rather an iterative process where further insights into the problem domain are to be continually contemplated. As an example, Reekie [32] defines the design process of a conceptual view in the following steps:

1. Create an initial conceptual architecture from for a software system (or on the base of requirements).
2. Design the concept with a focus on the required functionality.
3. Develop it with emphasis on quality attributes.
4. Iterate over step two and three until the model is complete.

3.2.3.1.2 Module View

The focus of the module view lies in expressing the organization of a software system in the form of modules as well as their relations. It first outlines major design decisions like the topological array of the system in layers which are in turn subdivided into functional modules. The modules entail all functionalities which are required in the system itself, like libraries, developed code components, technologies, runtime environments and interfaces which vary in different methods. Through the modularization and the arrangement of functionalities into layers, the module view exhibits on the one hand a segregation of components and defines on the other hand components as well as their functional extent. Furthermore, it has a major impact on the implementation whereas the implementation may also have a subsequent impact on the modularization because of changes in the course of the development and vice versa. The module view is usually created at an early stage in a software project and is often used for early estimations regarding reusability, security, portability and project planning. Possible model interfaces as well as dependencies between modules in the form of block diagrams (e.g. UML block diagrams) are typically constructed in this view as well [30].

3.2.3.1.3 Process View

The process view can be drawn in several layers of abstraction and generally show the logical path used by a system to obtain the capabilities which it is intended for. In other words, in the process view, the functionality of logical components are executed in succession to each other in order to create an appropriate result based on the action of a user of the software system. This implies that each process contains at least one, or several subtasks and several sub processes, which may be combined into one overall process, depending on the level of abstraction. The combination of all the processes outline the overall functionality of the software system. The process view shows the sequence of all tasks and process steps together with their interactions, which are usually called "messages". It is also possible to model non-functional requirements in the process view, such as performance or availability. One common scheme used in order to draw a process view is the widely renown UML notation. However, in the recent years the BPMN (business process management notation) also established itself as a common technique to describe processes, besides to UML. Compared to other software products, this view is important for information systems like CBS, as they basically process data over a given set of processes on demand of a user. Therefore, for information systems it is especially important to take all required processes into account and gather them in the process view [30].

3.2.3.1.4 Physical View

Essentially, the physical view describes how a software system is dispersed over the underlying hardware resources. The software is also taken into account as it influences the underlying infrastructure due to its need for physical resources. This relationship is two sided as the underlying infrastructure affects the deployed software and its abilities as well. In the physical view non-functional requirements like performance, scalability and availability are addressed along with an illustration showing which functional modules are deployed on which physical components. For instance, in the context of an information system, there are usually one or more databases deployed on a database server, which in turn run on a dedicated (virtual) server. In some cases, specifically smaller information systems with smaller amounts of data, the database server is also combined with an application server. The application server is also deployed on its own server with the database and the application server usually communicating over a network where enquiries are sent to a database and the responses are returned to the sender. The application server also communicates with clients (Webserver) over a network or the internet via TCP and Web Services. This means, that the entire functionality of the described information system is dispersed over three different servers which may be regularly backed up, replicated and can also run in several instances. Between them there may also exist firewalls and further infrastructure which affects the functionality of the system and therefore must be considered in the physical view [30].

3.2.3.1.5 Scenarios

In the context of Kruchten's 4+1 model, scenarios are instances of use cases. They are the collection of all possible use cases a system should be capable of handling in a standard environment and in the case of any error. They define what process must be carried out if a user performs certain actions in order to execute the requested task. This view works as a connector between the four previously described views as the use cases define the basis of all architectural elements, entities and their relationships. The use cases can also be seen as a functional arrangement of processes to achieve the requirements which had been prerequisite for the system. Therefore, they are a basis for a validation of the given software architecture [30].

3.2.3.1.6 Connections and Remarks

As Illustration 1 shows, the four components are connected to each other. The conceptual view influences the process view as the conceptual entities are mapped to respective processes, where they either process other entities or are processed themselves. The conceptual view also influences the model view, as the architectural entities need to be cast into modules depending on their size and functional volume. Finally, the module view and the process view affect the physical view because the deployment of functional modules and processes make up the majority of the content in the physical view.
In general, Kruchten's 4+1 model [30] is a basic view oriented approach to document a software architecture and shows a software architecture from different points of view. However, it may be an advantage to extend it with further views, as not all architectonic aspects of a software project are addressed within the basic model. A few instances include security aspects, the user interface, testing but also necessary upgrades, which in turn is tightly linked to the adaptability of the design principle.

3.2.3.2 Architectural Styles and Principles

In general, there are different metrics which define the quality of a software architecture. According to Bass et al [56], they can be roughly classified into metrics which are visible during the runtime and those which are invisible. Visible metrics consist of the performance, which is not only determined through the choice of underlying technologies and the hardware infrastructure, but also through their style of communication between each other as well as the segmentation of software modules. Other traits include security as well as the availability (in terms of fault tolerance, and communication security) of a product are attributes which can be used as a basis to evaluate the quality of a software architecture. Furthermore, the usability, which is in turn influenced by the above mentioned metrics, is also an aspect which is strongly affected by the underlying architecture and is therefore an indicator of its quality. The invisible attributes, like the modifiability of a product is determined by the degree of modularisation of a product's sub-components as well as their encapsulation. In addition to this, the portability and the reusability of software components also allow for deductions to be made about the quality of the architecture. Aside from that, the integrability and the extent to which a software is able to interact with external components as well as the overall testability of a product provide implications of its architectural quality. However, with the ongoing trends in the field of software engineering, especially in the field of cloud computing and distributed systems, more architectural quality aspects come into effect, such as the overall flexibility and the scalability of a software architecture. Sustainability and dependency on various technologies plays an increasingly important role for software architectures in general.

Except from attributes which are of crucial importance for a software architecture, architectural styles defining the fundamental structure of software components as well as their interactions can also affect the quality of an architecture [64, 65]. An architectural style generally consists of different design elements, depending on the type of architecture. For instance, a data-centered architectural style contains databases and data stores within its repertoire of design elements, while an architectural style showing data flows contains elements depicting data transmissions from one component to another one. These design components are partially motivated by design constraints, which describe how they may be combined with each other. Furthermore, these components also contain a semantic interpretation, which complies to the given constraints. To check architectural styles for consistency it is necessary to assess them with different analytical methods in order to verify their validity. An architectural style demonstrates a basic structure for an architecture which connects its content with an appropriate depiction of an associated method of construction. In the recent years, architectural styles have been significantly changed through the ongoing development of software and its environment in general.

However, Shaw and Garlan [33] defined a set of common architectural styles which are still widely used and will be briefly described in the following section.

3.2.3.2.1 Data centered Architecture

Data centered architectures mainly focus on the access of a number of clients to a central data repository. The data repository may be either realized as a passive variety, or as an active style. An example of a passive repository is a database which is queried by the clients, while an active repository sends notifications to its clients. The main advantage of an active data repository is that it is independent from its clients and functions as an autonomous system. Users referred to as subscribers, can be dynamically added, changed or removed. The active repository itself may also be modified as long as the communication interface and method of communication with its clients remains unchanged. Furthermore, this type of database enables clients to work in parallel without facing concurrency problems, as an active repository triggers outgoing events based on its inner state instead of being triggered externally by its clients. Additionally, these databases are easily scalable due to the flexibility granted to the clients. However, depending on the number of clients, structural changes in the communication may become costly, as they also have to be implemented for existing clients [21, 86].

In contrast to active repositories, passive data repositories are inquired by their clients which means, that the repository is triggered through external events and delivers a respective result. The main advantages of this style is, that the central deposition of data can be easily back upped, and the clients are to a certain degree capable of scalability as well as reusability, since they do not directly interact with each other. Another advantage of these databases is the reduction of data traffic through communication channels to the amount which is necessary at a given time, instead of broadcasted data traffic which is sent through active repositories. The drawback of passive repositories is that dependencies between the repository and its clients are much higher which results in structural changes within the repository often affecting the clients as well. Also the number of inquiries from the clients to the repository as a central data store may cause performance problems as well as concurrency difficulties.

3.2.3.2.2Dataflow Architectures

Dataflow Architectures [21, 75] are based on systems, which take a certain amount of data as input, transform it within one or several steps and create an output, based on the input and the internal transformation logic. The main aspect in terms of data flow architectures is the reusability as well as the modifiability of the transformation process, as it is on the one hand repeatedly applicable to several inputs and on the other hand the logic may be altered depending on its purpose. Dataflow architectures can be split into two sub-branches, Batch-Sequential (BS) data flows and Pipe-and-Filter (PF) data flows. BS data flows consist of several subcomponents, which work independently from each other. They regularly check whether an input set is available and process it according to their functionality. Afterwards they store the result to a location which is continuously monitored by the next subcomponent. In this manner, input data is transformed in several steps and delivered to an output location. The difference between BS and PF data flows is, that the components of BS data flows wait until its predecessor is finished with its task and created its result in its entirety, before beginning to process the given result. In contrast PF already begin to process input data as soon as parts of it are available, regardless whether the predecessor is finished or not. An example for BS data flows are Windows Batch Jobs, which execute a series of commands or transformation, based on a given Batch Script. However in Unix systems it is possible to pipe various commands together simultaneously, hence they are executed according to the P-F scheme.

```
tr 'A-Z' 'a-z' <fnord.txt | tr -cs 'a-z' '\n' | sort | uniq | comm -23 - /usr/share/dict/words
```
[87]

PF architectures are considered to be easier to implement and maintain in comparison to BS architectures. The reason for this is due to their defined connections and missing complex component interactions. They are also dependent on the same manner of data representation (usually in the form of ascii digits) and their performance is often not optimal. Also they are prone to Deadlocks, in case a predecessor is not able to finish its work properly or in a certain interval of time. In contrast BS architectures consist of components that are more independent from each other and also allow a degree of interaction with each other. However their subcomponents are required to wait until their predecessor finishes their tasks and outputs the result. This creates more modularity but also slows down the entire process in comparison to PF architectures.

3.2.3.2.3 Virtual Machine Architectures

The Virtual Machine architectural style is, unlike Cloud Computing, an architectural realization principle which roots further back to the beginning of high-level programming languages. In general, this style aims to abstract software functionality from the underlying platform on which it is running. That means, that a software package shall be made independent from the platform on which it runs. To do so, it is encapsulated into a virtual machine, which covers all platform specific aspects of the infrastructure and offers a common interface to the software running on it. One of the most well-known examples for Virtual Machine architectures, are programs written in Java. Depending on the Operating System (OS) on which a Java program is executed, it is embedded into a Java Virtual Machine (JVM). It acts as an adapter between the program and the underlying platform. The Java Runtime Environment (JRE) contains a number of JVMs, where each one is compatible with the specific settings of common operating systems like Windows, Unix or Solaris. The main advantage of this approach is that the Java program itself is platform independent and may be run on different operating systems without the need to be recompiled (as is the case for programs which are e.g. written in C/C++). The drawback of VM architectures is that the Virtual Machine usually consumes a certain amount of the system's resources, which decreases the performance of the application compared to applications which are specifically compiled for a certain OS. However, as the amount of resources available continues to incessantly increase over decades, the performance difference becomes more and more negligible [21, 76].

3.2.3.2.4 Call and Return Architectures

Call and Return Architectures are a basic architectural style for software in general, as they are widely used, particularly with the introduction of imperative and object oriented programming languages. They can be divided into four sub branches which will be described briefly in the following paragraphs [21]:

1. Main Program and subroutine architectures: They are used in all programming languages which are capable to outsource services into subroutines. Here a program consists out of a main routine which initially "owns" all logic as well as the data which is to be processed. In the course of its runtime it may call subroutines containing a defined part of the programs overall functionality once or repeatedly. Depending on the subroutine, arguments from the calling mother routine can be accepted and results may be returned either to the

calling procedure or to the system on which they run. This kind of architectural style also supports hierarchies of routines as each subroutine may in turn call further subroutines.

2. Remote Procedure Call Architectures (RPC): Are in principle the same as subroutine architectures, with the main difference that remote procedures are stored on different computers which are connected through a network. This architecture allows for the resources which are necessary to execute a program to be dispersed over several nodes. Another advantage is the possibility to support asynchronous procedure calls, which in turn offer the ability to execute code in parallel. Furthermore, the decoupling of code components over several computers enhances the physical independence of program modules with all its further implications, ranging from the realization of modules in different programming languages to technological decoupling.

3. Object oriented Architectures: Are currently the most widely used program paradigm in high-level computer languages. This style of architecture is mainly known for its encapsulation of data as well as logic into objects, that are only accessible through defined interfaces. Various concepts have been developed for object oriented architectures. Both Polymorphy (via reusability) and inheritance architectures are well known examples of this style. However, its main objective is to hide information and behaviour from the external environment and to offer its services as a black box to outside components which may call services and functions implemented in the internal structure.

Layered architectures: Are schemes where each layer builds on the layers beneath it and is used by the layers on top of them. Defined interfaces allow the communication between the layers which are all respectively based (and therefore dependent) on underlying layers. In the context of Remote Procedure Architectures, the behaviour as well as the data of the underlying layer is encapsulated and hidden from the overlying layer which calls the layer below it through public interfaces, in order to use the procedures available and receive results based on inputs. Layered architectures are often used in larger software projects and IT infrastructures as they provide the aptitude to physically separate, overlay and reuse layers. A common example for a layered architecture is the MVC pattern which will be described in chapter 3.2.3.3.5. A major advantage is the flexibility and modularity which is offered through this architecture. It makes software more maintainable as the usage of common interfaces as well as the horizontal architectural separation facilitates the exchange and modification of functional components and also enhances its portability. Unfortunately, every architecture still retains weaknesses and the main disadvantage of this principle is that overlying layers should only communicate with immediately underlying layers, implicating losses in terms of performance. Aside from that, there are systems in which layered architectures are not always applicable as they may be modelled in a manner that is incompatible with layered architectures.

3.2.3.2.5Independent Component Architectures

Independent component architectures [21] consist out of a number of processes and components, which interact with each other but are nevertheless independent. There are different substyles of this kind of architecture. As an example, an event based architecture contains a publisher component, which regularly sends messages to subscribed clients. If a client is interested in the messages from a particular publisher component, they register themself for a subscription by sending a subscription message to the event system. In this message they specify which information they are interested in. Subscribers may also act as a publisher for other messages by sending messages to an event system. The event system itself is a central component which receives messages from a publisher and notifies other registered clients about the new message. An advantage of this approach is that message providers and clients are decoupled from each other. Additionally, they are also enabled to run independently from each other and are not affected by one another, due to the asynchronous style of communication. From a systemic perspective, the system as a whole is easily extendable and maintainable as existing clients may simply be exchanged and new subscribers can be added to the system by simply registering themselves at the event system.
Another style of independent component architectures are components interacting with each other without a mediator. They are usually processes which run independently from each other and communicate directly through sending either synchronous or asynchronous messages. A common example for this paradigm are client server systems, where a server is inquired through one or several clients and responds accordingly after processing the request. Communicating processes and the publish subscribe paradigm are based on the concept that both communicating nodes acknowledge one another, but are still independent and separated, assuming that the communication style is asynchronous. A special case of communicating processes are peer-to-peer networks, where every node within the communication network is equal. That means that each node has a client- as well as a server function towards other nodes. Each node offers a set of services to the public which may be used by other nodes as well, through sending a request to the respective node. There are various protocols on different levels supporting this style of architecture, like the synchronous protocol TCP, as well as UDP, which is asynchronous. On a software level numerous protocols like RMI, CORBA and Remote Procedure Calls are commonly used.

3.2.3.2.6 Heterogeneous architectural Styles

In general software architectures are often combined within a single software product or module. As each paradigm exhibits both advantages and disadvantages, software architects usually try to combine them in a way to fit the requirements of a project as good as possible. For instance, client server systems are common in modern software engineering as well as layered architectures. Many technologies exist today which have already been implemented using a combination of architectures, which in turn indicates that every framework in which they are used is also subjected to those architectures. Due to the obvious advantages, a so called heterogeneous architectural style is used in the majority of software products. According to Bass et al [33], the architectural heterogeneity may be classified into three branches, namely domain dependent heterogeneity, hierarchy dependent heterogeneity and simultaneous heterogeneity. In terms of domain dependent heterogeneity, the architecture differs depending on subsystems or submodules of a software. This implies that a software persists as a combination of various submodules covering certain domains of its functionality and may be implemented in different architectures and technologies. As an example, a dispersed system may be deployed on two different servers which use different operating systems. Likewise, the respective submodules may be implemented in different programming languages, which already differ architecturally due to their technological nature (e.g. Python is architecturally different than Java, as Python supports not only the imperative and object oriented programming paradigm but also functional programming). Nevertheless, they are better able to realize the required functionality of the software product's submodules. However, as a consequence the product in its entirety is architecturally heterogeneous over its subdomains. Hierarchy dependent architectures emerge through the use of different architectures that are embedded into an overall architecture. An example would be a software framework consisting of several modules, which communicate via an asynchronous messaging system with each other (communicating process style). Each submodule may have a different sub-architecture, but is embedded into the overall architecture and therefore hierarchically subordinated. An example of simultaneous heterogeneity would be architectural styles which may be implemented in different ways. A layered architecture where a software is divided into software layers with abstract functionality from an underlying layer towards a superior layer can also be described as a kind of virtual machine architecture resulting from this abstraction.

3.2.3.3 Patterns

After common architectural principles were outlined in the previous chapter, this chapter will focus on the basic design patterns which play an influential role in the majority of software products of the recent decades [59, 60, 61]. In general patterns are reusable solutions to problems in terms of software engineering, which occur in different applications. In that context, they are technology independent best practices for recurring problems regardless of the utilized framework, programming language or application purpose. Software patterns are divided into design patterns and architectural patterns, whereas design patterns act on a smaller scale then architectural patterns. While design patterns are intended to solve code-level problems (e.g. Object Factories, Singletons, Iterators etc.), architectural patterns are focused on high-level architectural strategies impacting the entire software system. Accordingly, architectural patterns have a high impact on Core Banking Systems as they define to a large extent the architectural structure of a CBS and its submodules [122, 123]. While most CBS are structured in a layered architecture (like MVC as described in section 3.2.3.3.5) they also use patterns like the Master-Slave pattern or the Broker pattern. Therefore, the most important architectural patterns are outlined in the following.

3.2.3.3.1 Proxy

Proxies [21] impose a more or less public domain functionality to a server. They conceal a server and offer the same interface of the server to a domain of clients. In that way, they can be seen as a placeholder for the server in a client-server style communication pattern. The main advantage of the proxy scheme lies on the one hand in the decoupling of the clients and a server, and on the other hand on the "hiding effect". Through hiding the server behind a proxy, the server may be deployed in a different physical location then the clients, while the proxy offers its functionality to clients. Furthermore, the clients cannot directly access the server and therefore their access limits can be controlled by the proxy. For instance, the proxy can conduct preliminary and subsequent processing on each request of a client and is able to impose certain control mechanisms, in order to verify client's requests, or to limit their quantity.

However, a proxy should fulfil a number of constraints and it should take into account that it must not directly influence the communication between clients and the hidden server. First, it should be runtime efficient in order to avoid latencies in the communication. Second, its access should be transparent to the client side and it should offer the same interface as the server does, in order to prevent the call routine on the client side from the requirement to be altered. Also in most cases, the connection between the proxy and the server is a 1:1 relation, while the connection between the proxy and the client side may be a 1:n relation. There are in general various kinds of proxies fulfilling different responsibilities but act roughly according to the same principle. To them belong Remote Proxies, Protection Proxies, Cache Proxies, Synchronizations Proxies, Counting Proxies, Virtual Proxies or Firewall Proxies. Illustration 2 outlines the universal structure of a proxy pattern.

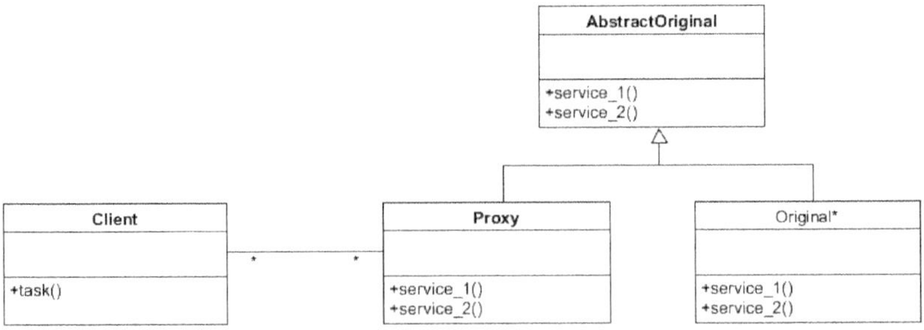

Illustration 2: The Proxy Pattern

3.2.3.3.2 Broker

A Broker [21] pattern works in the context of a dispersed system, where decoupled and often technologically heterogeneous components interact with each other. Its main advantage lies in the structuration and coordination of the components' (clients) communication where it forwards enquiries and responses as well as exceptions in the case of an error. In doing so it poses a single point of access, which identifies all services that are offered within its scope and offers them as an interface to other components. In this regard, it should be able to handle components that require access to other components. Furthermore, it should also be able to deal with components, which are edited, added or removed from a system during its runtime and it should be able to obscure system or technological details of the components from each other. These requirements are met with the introduction of an interface of a service for the public, which may then be accessed by various components, whereas technological heterogeneity like different implementation languages, different component architectures, or a different physical location must not affect the execution of tasks. To be more specific, a broker is publicly known in a system or at least within its scope. If a new component (server) is added to the system, it first registers itself as well as its services with the broker in order to be recognized and accessible within the broker's domain. If a client then requires a service, it sends its request to the broker, which forwards it to the registered server and returns the respective response. Through this concept it is possible to change system components during runtime as the components do not have to interact directly with each other. Additionally, in case a service is not available the broker can handle the exception and notify the calling client respectively without the system failing. Therefore, a broker enhances a system's flexibility and agility. Broker systems also emphasize system portability by concealing operating system specific details of a client from other clients, since it offers only indirect interfaces like application programming interfaces (APIs) to each client. Due to this, the client does not know which platform or which kind of network another client is operating in. In the case that a broker system is migrated from one platform to another, it is only necessary to adapt the broker and its interfaces to the new platform. Aside from that, brokers are able to interact with each other through the use of bridges (assuming they use the same protocol) which emphasizes the reusability of already used components.

3.2.3.3.3Master-Slave

A Master-Slave [21] system is a topology where one master controls one or several slaves. The slaves are identical and various assigned tasks are first sent to the master, who then dispatches them among the slaves. In this architecture, the master poses an interface to external components, in which the offered services are accessible. As soon as a service is called, the master splits the requested task into several subparts, which are then assigned to the slaves. They calculate an intermediate result, which is then assembled by the master to an overall result. In general, this approach enhances fault tolerance and parallel processing as well as an increased calculation accuracy. In addition to receiving tasks and dispatching their subtasks to the slaves, the master also maintains the slaves according to the "divide and conquer" principle. Illustration 3 shows a component diagram of a master slave architecture.

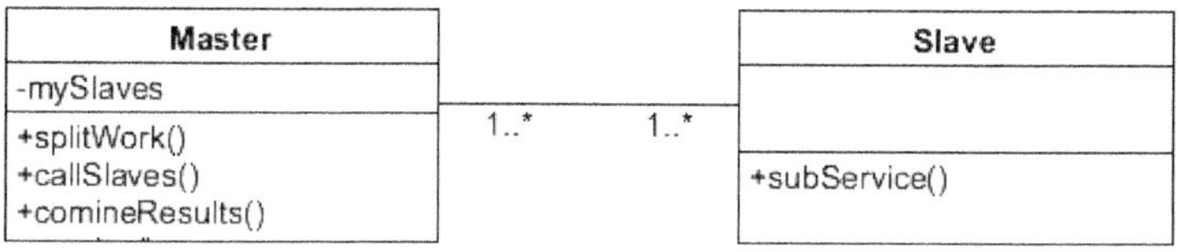

Illustration 3: The Master-Slave Pattern

Slaves may also be capable of conducting certain processes and are able to be realized as threads. Under certain circumstances, it is possible that slaves are dependent on each other, which means that a slave has to wait for a particular condition to arise, or for an argument from another slave. In this case it is necessary to interrupt ongoing calculations within the master slave architecture, in order to perform synchronization measures. However, it should be noted that this may lead to performance losses. In general, it is advantageous to define a slave as an abstract class in order to enable changeability and extendibility when implementing classes. Also, by segregating the executing code (slave) and the delegation code (master) it is easier to manage slaves and to create-, or provision slaves on demand. The main advantage of this principle is the aptitude to compute tasks in parallel, which increases performance as well as system efficiency significantly.

3.2.3.3.4 Client-Dispatcher-Server

A client dispatcher server pattern [21] is a naming service which is introduced as an intermediate layer between a client and a server, where it veils the details of a communication mechanism between a client and a server. The problem which is addressed through these mechanisms are distributed server networks, where a client calls a server usually by its name and the offered service. In any case, a server component should offer a service independent from its physical location or the location where it is deployed. Furthermore, the functionality of a product should be decoupled from the required functionality to access the product's services. By inserting a Dispatcher between a client and a server, the client is enabled to access the server via a given name, which is then resolved through the dispatcher, instead of accessing it directly through its absolute physical address. In addition, the dispatcher is also responsible for the maintenance as well as the creation of a connection between the client and the server. There are several kinds of Client Dispatcher Services, such as dispersed Dispatcher Services in which each Dispatcher does not know all addresses to servers but has knowledge of all other dispatchers within a network. In case a client wants to establish a connection to a server which is not known by an initial dispatcher, the connection is established though a dispatcher which knows the details of the desired server. This connection is then returned from the target dispatcher to the initial dispatcher and forwarded to the requesting client. Another type of dispatcher service returns the physical address of a requested server and leaves the maintenance of the connection to the client. Dispatcher services with heterogeneous communication styles store the protocols under which a server is able to communicate. In some cases dispatcher servers offer service titles instead of server names. That means, that a client does not address a specific server in order to get their request completed but a service, which implies the advantage that several physical servers may be attached to a service in order to provide redundancy in case of a server failure.

The general advantage of server dispatchers is the indirect access of clients to servers as well as the independence from physical addresses. This enables servers to be exchanged if necessary and their physical location is made imperceptible to the client. Also through the provisioning of services to clients it is possible to create redundancy, which in turn raises the availability of a certain functionality to the clients. Nevertheless, a drawback is that a dispatcher poses a single point of failure as a central component in this architectural pattern.

3.2.3.3.5 MVC

The MVC (Model-View-Controller) pattern [21] is a common design pattern in the context of software architectures. Often software products consist out of three parts, namely a user interface (view) defining the method of contact between the program and the user, a business logic (controller) that entails the behaviour of a software and a data domain (model) which outlines the data domain in which a program operates in. In general, MVC means that a program is divided into these three aspects which are then connected with each other through defined interfaces. Today many industrial software products are architecturally designed using MVC or in a style similar to MVC. The view is usually defined through a client framework, the controller is often realized in the form of an application server and the data model is usually depicted within a database. The main advantage of MVC is the enhanced maintainability of a software as the defined interfaces make it rather easy to replace software components, or even one of these three sections entirely. That means that either a client, an application server or a database with its model classes may be replaced. It is also possible to run several instances of a segment in parallel, which in practice, is mainly the client (E.g. if an application contains several clients for several kinds of users). In the context of CBS MVC architectures are often used where customers are offered a browser based client with the functionality for internet banking, while bank clerks are provided with an installed client which has more functionality in order to cover their business use cases.

4 Modernization of Core Banking System Architectures

This chapter outlines the modernization of software architectures from a number of views. First selected scientific approaches will be presented. Afterwards the BIAN as a more practical, but nevertheless generic approach will be discussed. Next, the architectures of selected existing CBS architectures will be summarized and evaluated and finally an exemplary CBS architecture will be outlined, which is the basis for chapter 5.

4.1 Modernization Approaches for Software Architectures

The modernization of software as well as software architectures is a particularly specific aspect in the field of software engineering. It is driven by the necessity to update technologies and architectures used in software frameworks in order to enhance their functionality and reduce risks connected to the use of old technologies and architectures. As software architectures define the structure of software frameworks, the modernization of software (code) is closely associated with the modernization of software architectures and therefore cannot be separated from each other. Fortunately, various approaches in order to evolve and modernize architectures have been developed in recent decades. They range from modernization roadmaps, via architecture-driven modernisation frameworks and architectural migration models, to knowledge based evolution frameworks. In the following sections, three exemplary approaches will be addressed, which shall give an overview of the architectural modernization approaches.

4.1.1 Architecture Options Workshop (AOWS)

The AOWS is based on the work of Ernst et al [34] which was published at the 13th Working IEEE/IFIP Conference on Software Architecture in 2016. It focuses on the planning phase of an architecture modernization, in which stakeholders often display great difficulty in the creation of an architectural target roadmap on the base of an existing system. According to Ernst et al, this trend was observed in practice during three modernization projects of three different architecturally outdated software frameworks between 2013 and 2016. The modernization was conducted by three different major organizations in the governmental and private sectors.

The entire approach is designed in an iterative way where each repetition consists of four parts. First, various architectures are selected, based on the risks and the business goals under which the modernization must takes place. Out of the designated architectures a single target architecture shall be selected through trade-off analysis and prioritization according to predefined criteria. In the selection process the decisions need to be documented along with the rationale why this architecture was selected, using a comparison between the implicated costs and advantages. Next, the selected choices shall be prioritized and chronologically ordered in preparation to execute them in the course of the roadmap. In its methodology the AOWS consists out of seven steps, which are assembled into three phases. The first phase is the so called "Preparation phase" where initially the business goals, which are to be fulfilled through the architectural modernization, shall be agreed upon. Scenarios are then composed for each goal in order to make it possible to achieve the predefined business goals. Within the second phase (Breadth - phase), each scenario must be examined on its own and certain architectures are to be defined, which would enable the modernization team to realize the scenario. As every architecture is a possible suitable candidate, the costs and benefits for each option need to be recorded in the scenario in which it is used as the foundation of an architecture. In the third phase (Synthesis - phase), the best architectural options shall then be prioritized and combined in a manner that will fulfil each business goal. This combination is then put together to a common roadmap which realises all given business goals. During the prioritization of options through a cost-benefit methodology, the participating stakeholders are asked to rate each cost and benefit on a High-Medium-Low scale. The thresholds between the three classes were set based on individual criteria. The prioritization of options may prove to be complicated, as each option may contain various dependencies as well as implications. Decision trees were used in order to cope with this challenge.

The creation of the roadmap depends on the number of business goals which are to be fulfilled and the timeframe over which the roadmap extends. However, the authors of the AOWS approach recommend that the roadmap's timeframe should remain below a two-year time limit and its progress should be regularly reviewed. If a modernization process of a software is estimated to take more time than two years it is considered practical to split the modernization into several intermediate-term phases, whereas each one is covered by its own roadmap. Furthermore, in practice modernization processes of software products are often subject to exogenous influences such as funding, organizational- as well as business constraints. These circumstances need to be considered in the development of the roadmap, and its sub-steps (Milestones) must be planned accordingly. Each Milestone is marked with a due date until which a sub-step must be completed.

4.1.2 Model Driven Software (Architecture) Modernization

Model Driven software modernization [45, 46] is a common approach in terms of the evolution of legacy systems to a more up-to-date framework. Due to its popularity, several approaches have been developed, ranging from reverse model engineering (in order to extract a language independent model from an existing system) to the semi-automated implementation of new code under a new architecture, using the previously gained model. One approach is the Model Driven Architecture, which was adopted by the Object Management Group in 2001. This methodology became one of the central concepts in the context of model driven development, as it defines the core principles of software- and architecture modernization using model driven means. Other software modernization approaches (e.g. Fuentes-Fernández et al [37, 48, 49] with his proposed XIRUP – eXtreme end-User dRIven Process) use MDA to cover the architectural aspect of their modernization projects.

The main goals of the MDA approach is to guarantee the portability, interoperability and reusability of a software product through the separation of its behaviour from its design as well as its architecture. That means that the description of functionality in terms of architecture and design is made independent from the technology and the platform on which it is implemented. A main concept of MDA is that the model operates as a formal description of the function and the structure of the underlying code. To achieve this goal, the MDA approach usually utilizes UML (unified modelling language) as a common description notation.

The MDA process itself contains several steps in order to transform a source system from a source target into a target system on a respective target platform. The first step is to abstract the source system into a UML based platform independent model (PIM). The PIM omits the technical details of a system that are related to its platform and thereby separates the source system from the platform on which it is deployed. The PIM then serves as a source model, which is transformed into a target model through the application of defined transformation rules.

The next step involves the creation of the target model which, according to the MDA standard, is platform specific (PSM) and hence already customized in order to fit the specifics of a target platform. That means, that the PSM has to combine the functional specifics of the PIM, adapted through transformation rules, with all details about its use of the planned target platform. As a third step the transformation rules, depending on the nature of the PIM as well as the PSM, need to be defined as they essentially provide mapping rules from entities and relations of the PIM towards a respective counterpart in the PSM. The transformation itself is aimed to be as automated as possible in order to reduce manual interference which may be prone to errors. However simply applying mappings from a PIM-root object to a PSM-target object is not enough to accomplish a complete transformation. Therefore, so called marks provide information about the way in which a certain entity should be transformed. Marks are platform specific and hence are a part of the PSM. One of the requirements of marks lies in the PIM-model elements which are applicable to a mark needing to be defined and the mappings in turn being defined in a dedicated mapping language. To satisfy this need, OMG adopted the so called MOF QVT language (Meta Object Facilities Query/View/Transformation). Illustration 4 depicts a high-level overview of the MDA transformation approach.

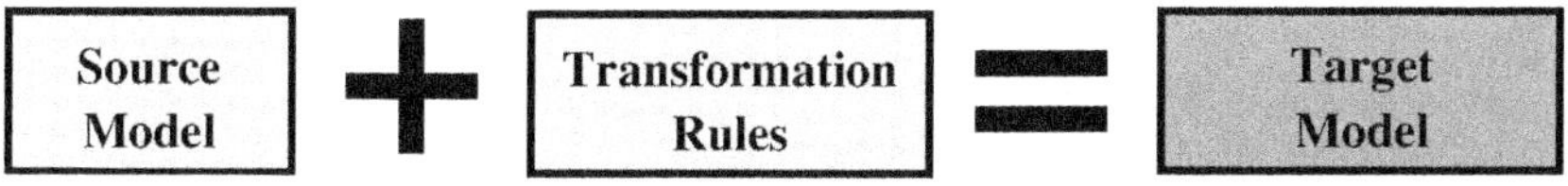

Illustration 4: Schematic Overview of the MDA approach

The fourth step is to generate code and "living" artefacts out of the target model. In practice frameworks might also be included, which support the automated abstraction of a source model out of existing code.

In general MDA is also capable of functioning as a modernization approach since the transformation rules also allow the transformation of a source model into a target model, which is structured in a more accurate and consolidated architecture. Therefore, in practice, it is possible to generate a PIM from different source code languages, as long as the languages utilize a common set of logical rules and structures (like logical branches, loops or operators). These rules are used to transform data and thus define the behaviour of a program. This behaviour may be abstracted (along with the architecture) into a PIM and separated from the underlying technology as well as the platform. As soon as a PSM is created, utilizing a suitable architecture and appropriate technologies, the transformation rules can be created. In relation to the code generator, it is possible to build a converter which automatically implements modernized code under a modernized architecture from an existing PIM. During that process, the transformation rules are the component among the MDA which entail the most testing, in order to prevent logical errors arising. A method of testing consists of running the code generated by the converter and to compare its behaviour to the behaviour of the original code. Usually an emulator has to be refined in several implementation runs, until it is able to reliably convert from one framework to another one. The main benefit of the MDA approach is the formal abstraction of the source code into a meta model, as it divides technologies and frameworks from behaviour and structure. On the one hand the PIM poses a detailed documentation of the source system and the on the other hand, it provides the capability of re-implementing it in any other language and in any other architecture, depending on the transformation rules.

4.1.3 Architecture-centric software evolution (ACSE)

The Architecture-centric software evolution approach (ACSE), is based on the work of Ahmad et al [36, 47], who adheres to a broader approach, focusing on a constant evolution of software architectures as a requirement to keep software continually adapted and usable. To realise this scheme, they propose a so called "PatEvol" Framework, consisting of a set of activities with the purpose to execute two main modernization steps. The first is the acquisition of Architecture Evolution Knowledge and the second one manages the application of the gained knowledge. The overall ACSE process is depicted in the following Illustration 5.

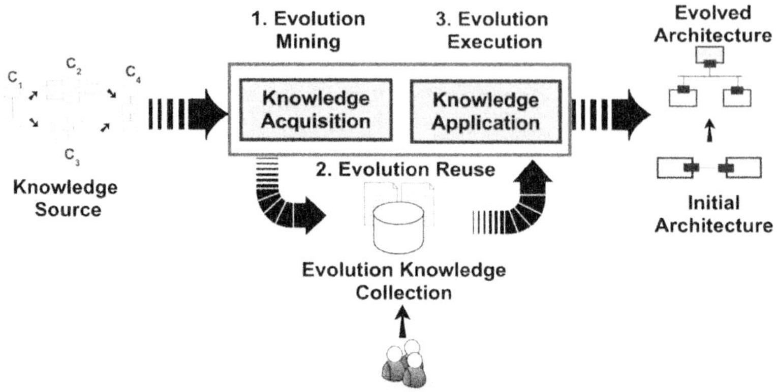

Illustration 5: The ACSE process

The source, which is necessary for developing an initial architecture into its next evolutionary stage, is an existing knowledge base which is realized in the form of a (software) repository where all architectural changes are consistently recorded. From there architectural change logs shall be used in order to conduct knowledge acquisition through evolution mining. Put simply, the change logs of the software repository will be examined for formal architectural changes. Common challenges in this context involve the size of change logs, as they may become large and could result in an analysis becoming extensively time consuming as well as the possibility of a manual inspection, which is likely to be error prone. In order to overcome these problems, a graph based change notation, derived semi-automatically from the logs, is recommended. Through the application of graph-mining techniques on the derived graph, recurring as well as nonrecurring architectural change patterns can be discovered. Subsequently, the changes must be taxonomically classified with the aim to serve as a foundation for further discovery and template based specification of evolution patterns. The classification is carried out through searching graph patterns which indicate commutative and dependent architectural changes. This approach is rather intuitive and requires details about the composition of the underlying history of previous structural changes.

Once the knowledge acquisition activities are completed, the derived evolution patterns are added to an evolution pattern catalogue which is represented in Illustration 5 above as the evolution knowledge collection. Through collecting the gathered patterns in a catalogue using a generic specification format, architects are enabled to reuse these patterns in the future in order to resolve

recurring architectural challenges faced in the overall evolution process. Furthermore, these patterns are based on the given piece of software, which signifies that they are already within the problem space as well as the context of the underlying software.
The second main step is the application of the gained architectural knowledge to the underlying software. In order to do so, an architectural evolution step (modernization) is formally specified according to given requirements. The specification contains three main sections: first, an appropriate description of the source architecture. Second, all constraints which impact the evolutionary step and third; the concrete steps in which a software component is either added, changed or removed with the aim to realize the software evolution. Within the specification, decision rationale behind the change as well as the scope of the modernization step must be outlined thoroughly. After the specifications are established, architectural evolution patterns need to be selected from the previously created pattern catalogue. They provide a mapping from the initial problem to a possible solution which is already within the specific domain of the software product. Ahmad et al propose to use a Question-Option-Criteria approach in order to find the suitable patterns for an evolutionary step, since the selection of architectural change patterns is a rather complex problem. Using this approach, first the pattern catalogue is queried with a certain problem or question. Ideally it delivers certain patterns as possible solutions to the specified problems and the most appropriate one is then selected, depending on how well it suits to the given criteria. Once all architectural change patterns have been selected, they are implemented on the software product. The resulting changes are recorded in the architecture change log with the purpose to serve as an information source for future evolutions.
In general, the ACSE approach does not focus on just one architectural modernization and hence is not seen as an atomic action. Instead, it focuses more on the overall evolution of a software product, which in turn is more beneficial for the lifecycle of long living software products that are enhanced over decades.

4.2 BIAN – A Standard for Modern CBS Software Architectures

The Banking Industry Architecture Network (BIAN) [95] is an independent organization which promotes the standardization of service oriented architectures in the banking sector. Having emerged out of the Industry Value Network (IVS), this institute aims to connect Banks and service providers as well as banking software vendors. The motivation of the organization is founded on the fact that requirements of banks towards their IT infrastructure, particularly the CBS, are constantly varying. Banks are subject to rapidly increasing external influences, which in turn implicates that they require a more flexible IT infrastructure in order to better provide the offered services at lower costs. The common challenges which banks face in terms of their IT infrastructures

lie in the fact that each bank has a unique IT landscape, which is usually slow and expensive to adapt and depicts a lack of interoperability. In order to provide a solution to that, BIAN seeks to standardize banking IT infrastructures on a service oriented basis. In general, BIAN adopts a service oriented architecture (SOA) and thus is formally named BIAN SOA Framework (currently in version 7). The rationale behind this approach is the topological separation of functionality into separate services. Through that topology an improved information flow and greater architectural flexibility is provided. The embedded functionality is also exposed and hence accessible to all other services as well as external components. Aside from that, through the reusability of services, the system is set up more efficiently which reduces software development and maintenance costs. Another advantage of the service oriented approach is that the services use messaging in order to communicate with each other, which indicates better security as well as monitoring facilities and enhances the architectural and functional flexibility significantly. Another benefit is the reduced complexity of the software as the functional composition of the services is not nested but instead situated on one general hierarchical level where no service encapsulates or controls another. Therefore, the entire system is less complex as the services are kept in a moderate functional size and are correspondingly easy to maintain and extend in the long term.
The core artefact of the BIAN is the service landscape, which defines an activity diagram for banking use cases and can be viewed as a standardized collection of banking services. Illustration 6 shows an overview over the BIAN service landscape and its service clusters.

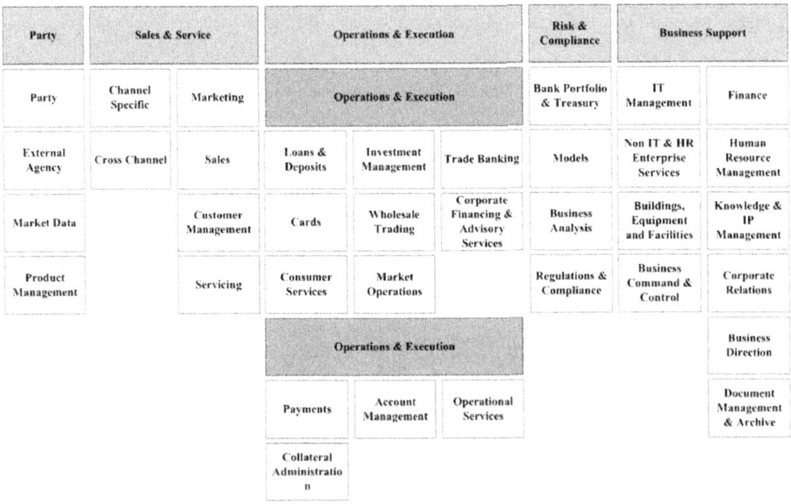

Illustration 6: The Overall Service landscape of the BIAN [88]

Each service in the service landscape is modelled in UML and does not focus on any technology or infrastructure in which a banking functionality should be realized, but rather depicts the procedure which should be adhered for the creation of a the same. An overview of important entities, and how they are organized among each other is also presented by this approach. The following example shows an exemplary scenario for credit assessment. It involves all stakeholders, who participate in the process and the respective sequential high level actions, which are necessary to complete a credit assessment [88].

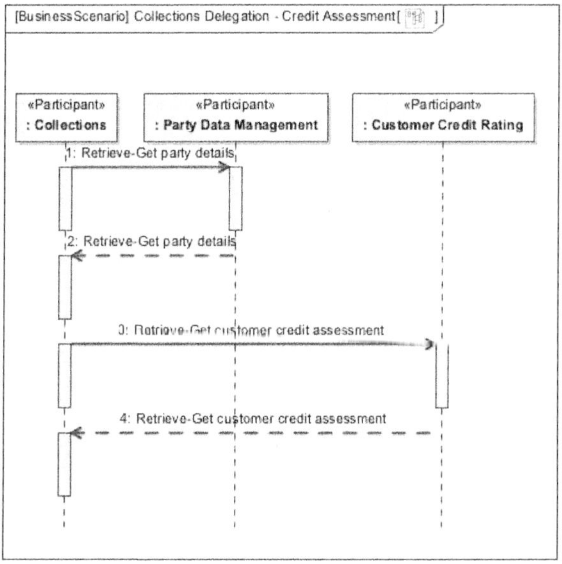

Illustration 7: Credit Assessment Scenario according to BIAN

In addition to the service landscape, BIAN entails a how-to guide, a meta-model, a set of business scenario definitions as well as a service domain definition, which are all complemented through a common BIAN business vocabulary. In that context BIAN defines three major components [88]:

- A service domain is a functional service or module. Each service domain has a unique business goal, and capabilities with each domain containing a set of activities which detail the formal realization of its semantic meaning (business goal). That means each service domain contains the 'What', the 'Why' and the 'How' of a business capability.
- A business domain is the next abstraction on top of the service domains and consists of a set of service domains. These domains summarize a number of business capabilities into

a broader business area and represent already standardized departments of a bank such as loan and deposit management, customer management or trade banking.

- Business domains are aggregated to business areas, which is the highest level of classification and can be seen as a business group of a bank such as services, risk and compliance, sales or business support.

Through the use of these three entities, BIAN tries to standardize the approach used by CBS vendors as well as banks for their IT-infrastructure. The main advantages which emerge from this procedure is that each vendor who complies with the standard modularizes Core Banking functionality according to the same pattern. In turn, that implies that software solutions (with partly disjoint functionality) are much easier to integrate, and obtain a higher application to application compatibility. Through the service oriented modularity, a greater flexibility is achieved as each service can be added, removed, updated or reused with less effort. The overall interoperability of a CBS is also enhanced, as third party functionality may be included into the framework as "just another service".

In terms of design principles, BIAN's central policy is the breakup of banking functionality into a collection of isolated and discrete services (service domains). Each service domain contains on the one hand an asset, and on the other hand a certain usage. Assets are essentially data that are modelled by using hierarchically ordered entities. The sum of the entities models the entire data domain of the bank, and likewise the information which is processed by a bank. Through the usage of the collection of the BIAN's services, a given entity or set of information are processed as necessary. Each service domain is elemental which means, that each service of BIAN's collection covers a certain business role and several services may be combined to fulfil a bigger purpose. In that regard, each service domain acts as a service centre, which means that each service is triggered on the basis of a request. The request asks the service to perform a task according to its given functionality and deliver a response to the client. Such a request could also require that the invoked service has to send further requests to other services in order to fulfil its task. The interaction between service domains is well defined and regulated using control records that connect the behaviour of a service with its output and logs its process. Within business scenarios the sum of service domains is described, which are used to cover the functionality of a business process, as well as their interactions with each other. They depict the service domains involved on a high level and represent the flow of information between them. According to the standard, the interactions are also described in semantic terms, in order to provide a consistent and unambiguous interpretation [88].

Another major principle of the BIAN standard is that it should be interpretable in different situations. This principle should be independent from technical environments and hence must be possible to implement with the use of various technologies, depending on the requirements of a bank.

There are two main methods of usage intended for the BIAN standard; first it can be used as a high level specification for a solution, with the capability to fulfil the main use cases of a bank. Second, it can be used as a blueprint for an existing system, in order to develop it towards the standard. To do so, BIAN is designed to be capable of being mapped to existing systems and services, which may either realize, or replace projected BIAN services. Its service landscape may also be translated or connected to other architecturally important models, such as process models or data models. In terms of interconnectivity BIAN's service domains contain a clear definition of their interfaces and their functional segments. This enhances their interoperability and flexibility massively as they may be used either in big legacy applications or within frameworks, where they are obligated to cooperate with other applications, or as a kind of black box within a multi-application cloud environment. In this regard BIAN may also be used to create a benchmark of an enterprise blueprint which stays constant over time. For instance, over the course of the years, it is possible that the function of a service domain may change. However, its business purpose and hence its semantic will remain the same. Through its stability, the BIAN service landscape is capable of being expended as a benchmark in order to verify the performance and compliance of existing systems to map-, and evaluate their existing coverage, and to create more fitting requirements through mapping needed functionality to the service domains of BIAN.

The BIAN service landscape covers a range of functionality as Business Areas, whereas each Business Area contains a set of Business Domains. Each Business Domain in turn consists of a set of Business Scenarios which are comprised of Services. The high level Business Areas covered by BIAN are defined as follows [88]:

- Reference Data: Contains the domains which are related to stem data and data exchange. Examples of these types of data include product data (Product Management), customer data (Party) as well as market data and modules which cover data exchange to external agencies like other banks and further third party related banks.
- Sales and Service: This Business area comprises all data which refers to customer contacts. It is organized in channels (e.g. ATM management, invoices or contact centres), cross channels (interactive customer help, authentication, or points of service), sales, marketing as well as customer management (e.g. credit rating, relationship management).
- Operations and Execution: this area entails the core components and operations of a bank. Product specific operations such as loans and deposits, bank cards, market operations, wholesale trading, investment management or trade banking are some of the operations included in this aspect. Furthermore, cross product operations like account management, payments, collateral administration or operational services are also a part of this Business area.

- Risk and Compliance: This area covers all business scenarios which have to do with risk in the wider context of banking like Bank Portfolio and Treasury Management, Business Analysis, Risk Modelling as well as legal regulations and compliance.
- Business Support: Consists out of all corporate related services which are not directly related to the added value of a bank. Instances of this include; the facility management, corporate relations, business command, finance, HR, the IT Management or the document archive.

As previously mentioned, the BIAN may be applied to banking IT infrastructures in three different ways, although it can be said that BIAN is not a modernization framework but rather a target architecture which should be fulfilled in the longer term. Nevertheless, it may be used as a high level implementation design for the creation of an enterprise blueprint and as a foundation for long term planning and analysis on existing IT infrastructures and CBS. However, as this procedure deals with the modernization of existing CBS, the main focus is on the third approach as the description of all three processes would exceed the scope of this thesis.
In the context of a target architecture one of the main advantages which make the BIAN standard attractive as a benchmark for CBS is the temporal stability it offers. Over time this results in the business purpose of each service remaining the same whereas only the technical method of implementation or the justification may need to be modified. Furthermore, it is independent of any organizational- or technical constraints as its services are modelled in a way which does not take implementing technology or underlying infrastructure into account. Therefore, the standard can be introduced into any technological environment that fits a consumer bank's requirements and offers the required functionality. In addition, service oriented functional granularity as well as the ability to map its standardized services to existing functional modules, and take the models of missing or outdated services as a high level design for future modules render the BIAN suitable for benchmarking purposes. The principal factor in order to comply with the BIAN is to adopt its organizational structure in terms of its proposed services, and to follow the activity schemes which are represented in each service. However, should a bank decide to develop its infrastructure towards the BIAN standard, several years will be required in order for the process to be implemented incrementally. The first step in order to determine the gap between the architecture of an existing CBS and the BIAN is to map existing functionality to the services of BIAN. It is also necessary to assess the existing functionality against the functionality of each mapped service from BIAN. This can be done both via the feature attributes of the target architecture as well as through the use of custom criteria which better fit the system properties or the business considerations of the using bank. This highlights another benefit of BIAN as the attributes of its service domains are not restricted to a certain set and may be extended with custom attributes, which in turn simplify the assessment of banks within the context of "their" performance indicators. For instance, the BIAN's How-to Guide proposes a quadrant ranking system in which service domains

are rated on their implicated knowledge distribution, in combination with the grade of their sourcing.
After the existing functionality has been benchmarked against the BIAN as a target architecture, it is necessary to define the steps which are to be taken to progress from the current architecture to a BIAN compliant structure. This is usually accomplished by selecting and executing one of the modernization approaches as discussed in chapter 4.1.
In order to track the progress, BIAN recommends to use the defined BIAN target architecture as a blueprint for measuring the technical as well as the business progress. The rationale behind this is, that BIAN's modules are isolated and work packages, or so called "units", are established which can be tracked from a project manager. Further business and financial related performance indicators may be attached to each service domain along with system related or non-system related costs. This allows project managers to trace costs during the modernization process down from a business perspective to a service perspective level.
Regarding the determination of functional gaps, the BIAN service domains offer a high level specification of missing services deemed necessary to gain needed functionality. They can then be elaborated according to specifications and the technologies that are utilized by a bank, or a CBS vendor.

4.3 Architectures of existing CBS

Usually CBS are grown systems which often contain technologically rather heterogeneous, old-fashioned and partially outdated technologies. Accordingly, detailed information about the core systems are kept confidential by the CBS vendors. However, public sources also give high level hints on how the architectures of certain vendors are structured. Some of them are described in the following subsections.

4.3.1 Avaloq

The Avaloq Banking Software Solution [80] descends from the Swiss BZ Bank and has its roots in the banking software "AdvAntAge" from it was developed in 1996. Since then Avaloq has developed into an independent company with more than 2200 employees and more than one hundred fifty customers in the financial sector who are dispersed over more than 25 countries. Aside from the smaller subsidiaries in ten countries, Avaloq also runs three development centres in Zurich and Edinburgh as well as a development support centre in Manila. In terms of functionality, the Avaloq banking system is segmented into 80 modules, which are grouped into five core components:

- Universal Banking

- Retail Banking
- Wealth Management
- Transaction Banking
- Central Banks

The architecture of this scheme is generally divided into three layers, that are superimposed upon each other, like the MVC model. According to the public web presence of the Avaloq Group [80], its Product is focused on efficiency, scalability and consistency. The top layer is the so called Avaloq Client Tier. It is partitioned into several clients, which are intended on the one hand for the employees of a bank, and on the other hand for the customers. The employee client ("Smartclient") is stated to be based on .net, which means that it is likely implemented in C#/.net in combination with various further .net based technologies. Additionally, the Avaloq Group offers a HTML 5 based Webclient, as well as an iOS App that can be installed on Apple products through the Apple's Appstore. The communication between the Client Tier and the Middle Tier is realized via Webservices, whilst the Middle Tier itself consists of an Integration Server (Windows Server) and a Linux based Avaloq Front End System. The middle Tier functionality is implemented in C#/.net and Java/EE. Below the Middle Tier, the Avaloq System encompasses the Backend Tier, which is the core of the system. It is deployed on a Unix Server and contains the data base, realized through an Oracle Database and accessed via PL/SQL. The three Tier architecture was selected by Avaloq in order to reduce the complexity of the architecture and concentrate the functionality in these three layers, which means that the services can be appropriately separated from each other. Above all, software flexibility in its vertical and horizontal scalability is the main purpose for the development of this architecture. Additionally, by standardizing the communication interfaces between these layers, it is comparably easy to add new use cases or functional modules to the Avaloq Banking System. According to Avaloq's Webpage, banking functions are realized in standardized business transactions and objects, which implies a structure in their entities and insinuates that the Avaloq Source code is (at least partly) object oriented. In order to implement new functionality, Avaloq uses a model driven approach, which means that through the help of source code independent modelling languages, a meta model of the new functionality is created. This model can be generated either from existing code or be written manually. Based on this model, it is significantly easy to rapidly create source code, which reflects the requested behaviour. The advantage of the model driven approach lies in the increased speed of development of code in a higher clarity and quality as well as less redundancy occurring in the code, according to the principle of "don't repeat yourself". The disadvantage in this method is the high initial effort, which is necessary in order to create a meta model of a (complex) software project. However, the initial code, which is the basis for the creation of the meta model, does not have to be object oriented. That means, through the concept of model driven development it is possible to (semi) automatically create new code parts, which obey modern code standards, out of (architectonically) old code components. This approach implies that the Avaloq Group solution is actually in a transformation process, where new clean and consistent business objects shall be created from old code on a step by step basis. An integration layer is used in parallel to the three tier architecture of the Avaloq Banking System. This layer contains integration services as well as adapters which build on technical standards and are intended to aid in the communication with third party business and infrastructure services, provided by customer banks. In order to extend Avaloq's model driven development approach, and to enable customers to parameterize the system according to their own requirements, Avaloq created the Eclipse based tool "ice Workbench". Through usage of this tool a customer bank is given the opportunity to define own business processes using the BPMN notation and DSL (domain specific languages). These BPMN created processes produce a meta model which is automatically implemented into the respective source code. Afterwards the source code can be versioned, compressed and, in form of customer internal releases, be integrated into the existing system.

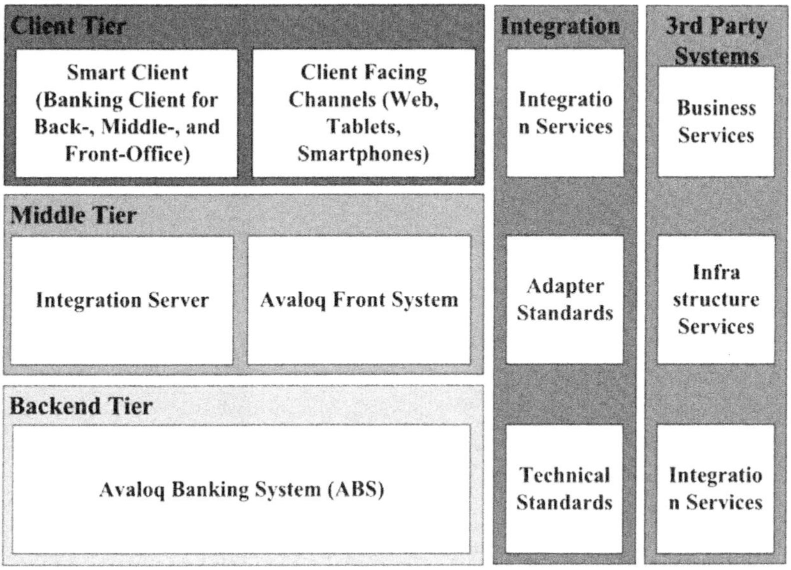

Illustration 8: The Overall Architecture of Avaloq [80]

4.3.2 Finnova

The Finnova AG Bankware [81] was developed by the Swiss company Finnova AG. Its roots date back to 1974 and the "FIS" banking software. The current Finnova Banking System, developed between 1999 and 2003, was intended as a modular built system for universal as well as private banks. The target market for the Finnova software is mainly situated in Switzerland and its neighbouring countries. Up until the present moment, the Finnova AG boasts about 400 employees and supports about 100 customer banks.

The fundamental architecture of the Finnova Bankware is similar to the architecture of Avaloq since it's architecture is also divided into three layers (Access Layer, Application Layer, Interface Layer) and that its focus lies on adjustability, and scalability. However, one difference between the architecture of Finnova and Avaloq is that an inquiry is not necessarily forwarded from the Frontend to the Backend and vice versa. Finnova's functionality is instead grouped into subdivisions which each consist of topologically similar functions. This implicates that each layer depicts a collection encapsulated of modules which enables customers to only integrate parts of the Finnova software into their existing IT infrastructure. Physically, the Server components (Application Layer and Interface Layer) seem to be deployed on an application Server from IBM (Server of the z/Series, whereas this Server series is a Mainframe Legacy System from the 1960s and 1970s).

The servers are equipped with an IBM-adapted Linux operating system, called AIX, which is essentially a front-tier and mid-tier server. Aside from that, the web presence of Finnova reveals that for data storage a database server, deployed with either an Oracle Solaris operating system or with Linux, is used for data storage. An Oracle 12 Instance is installed on this database server in order to manage the data repository. Furthermore, Finnova partially reverts to a Unix operating system, which was originally adapted by Hewlett Packard. In addition, the criteria of adjustability is realized through interfaces, which enables customers to adapt the CBS according to their own specific requirements. The factor of scalability is in all probability implemented through the activation of a sufficient number of server instances that are hosted on several physical servers and each separately communicate with the database.

The bottom layer (Interface Layer) is, according to Finnova's web presence [81], responsible for the communication between the software framework and external components. It is likely implemented in Java and uses a technology, created by the Finnova AG, called OPAL (Open Architecture Layer) in order to interact with other software components via a specifically designed SOA concept made of Web Services. The technologies which were used in the Interface Layer are XML interfaces as well as HTTP/HTTPS and PL/SQL interfaces. The XML interfaces are presumably responsible for the transmission of all XML based sub products of the MS Office Framework, especially generated documents. The ODBC connection, the Oracle Gateway (for the inclusion of foreign databases) and individual reports are likely supported by PL/SQL interfaces with further customized functions made available through APIs. These interfaces can be used by customers to create private in-house developments with the ability to interact with each other. This presents a feasible method for customers to adapt the systems to a certain degree and also a way for Finnova to transfer development work to the customer.

The Application Layer is also likely to be implemented in Java. It contains the functional modules of the CBS which are realized as processes or more specifically in process groups, and are embedded into a real time Kernel. The Realtime Kernel acts as the centerpiece of the system and encompasses the Front Office, via the Middle Office, to the Back Office and thus embraces the main processes of the Finnova Framework and is responsible for their control. It queries the modules periodically and is likely to control the communication between the submodules as well as the communication with external services. The architecture of the Finnova Application Layer is divided into processes and data (compare to Illustration 9), with the processes responsible for selecting, transforming and persisting data. For instance, the process customer stem data contains all customer data as well as the use cases which are necessary to handle customer data. All these processes which are depicted in Illustration 9 disembogue into the component central data storage which is likely a synonym for the database. The results of the processes Corporate Action, Settlement, Tax Statement and Securities are likely to be connected to a relational Data Warehouse, which is in turn connected with the database. The main advantage of the Data Warehouse is that through its entirety of data it is possible to derive key performance indicators, which are then used for a so called "Management Information System" (MIS). The MIS gives the management level of a customer bank the opportunity to extract financial indicators from the database, which are subsequently used as the basis for navigation measures. Also the results of the processes Stock, Loans, Payment Transactions and Treasury are aggregated to documents through an Output Management System, which in the technological aspect means that there must be a document generation frame-work within the Application Layer, in addition to a real-time-Kernel. Further software components exist in the Application Layer that cover various use cases like document viewing, scanning applications in order to process payment transactions et cetera.

The topmost architectural layer of the Finnova Framework is the Access Layer, through which customers as well as bank employees interact with the Banking System (Application Layer). The Access Layer accepts transactions from the following client groups:

- Workplace of the bank employee
- Bank counter
- Internet (e-Banking)
- Cashpoints

That means that the access layer runs at least three software clients:

- A browser based web client for E-Banking, which is capable of conducting account, saldo and booking transactions as well as the import and export of customer data. It can also communicate with the bank's server via Secure Mail and also supports transaction signature means such as smartcards, kobil-Sticks and mTans. The data communication with the server operates in real time and data is persisted in near real time in the database.

- A client for bank employees supporting cash and cashless use cases as well as an offline operating mode, which in turn leads to the conclusion that the client has the ability to store data temporarily and synchronize it with the servers at a later time.
- A client which is installed on cashpoint machines. It is likely to support services for the bank and external banks, like receipts, deposits and account transactions.

In addition to the clients, the Finnova framework also supports telephone banking, which enables customers to enquire account balances, transactions and the bank's business hours. Furthermore, the access layer contains a CRM (Customer Relationship Management) system, a PMS (Portfolio Management System), a loan consulting component and an OMS (order management system). The communication between the access layer and other components is carried out by interfaces that are realized by the Finnova OPAL technology, which is basically a web service following the SOA concept.

On the basis of its Interface Layer, Finnova also offers a variety of interfaces to external software components (Webservices, XML, APIs, etc.). In the technological aspect, the access layer is with likely implemented in Java and JavaScript (AngularJS) as well as HTML, which is realized with the aid of JSF and CSS. For the web client Finnova also uses JSON, Ajax and further Web Components. Illustration 9 depicts the high level architectonical structure of the Finnova Framework.

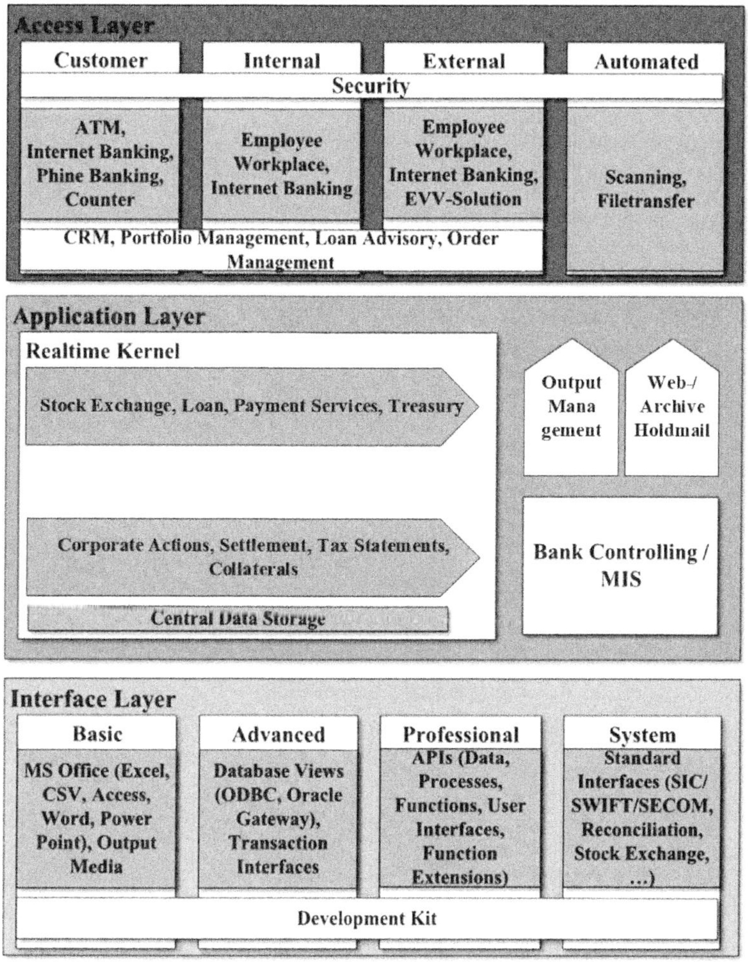

Illustration 9: Finnova's Overall Architecture [81]

4.3.3 Temenos

The Swiss company Temenos [82] was founded in the Year 1993 and established itself as a global vendor for Banking software. According to its own statements its frameworks are used by more than 3000 banks in about 150 countries, whereas 500 million bank customers use the software directly or indirectly in order to process bank actions and transactions. According to the architecture branch of its website it is architectonically focused on flexibility, performance and productivity as key principles. In a technical context, this means that the Temenos software has to be scalable in its functional spectrum but also in its physical performance in order to fulfil the mentioned characteristics. In terms of functionality, Temenos offers a wide spectrum and covers the following banking branches:

- Retail Banking
- Universal Banking
- Private Wealth Management
- Transaction Banking and Payments
- Microfinance
- Corporate Banking
- Credit Unions
- Insurance
- Islamic Banking
- Treasury & Capital Markets

According to its web presence, Temenos is split up vertically into Front Office, Middle Office and back office and also entails a Business Intelligence component. In order to maintain the Front End, Temenos uses a central Framework called Edge Connect UXP which realizes the functionality of the client. Connect UXP is a HTML based platform that is used to create browser based application. These applications (Internet Client and the Mobile Client of Temenos) represent the customer and bank communicating with the presentation layer of the Temenos software and are secured according to the OWASP standard. The communication with the layers beyond the presentations is realized through the Ajax concept (JavaScript and XML). With this framework, Temenos created three separated clients:

- Temenos Connect Onboarding
- Temenos Connect Mobile
- Temenos Connect Internet.

Using these three clients, customers can access their bank account over the internet from PCs, tablets and mobile phones. The clients communicate with the T24 Core Banking Framework, which is likely implemented in Java. The T24 Framework is structured in a functionally modular-, as well as a service oriented way and plays the role of the core component of the entire Temenos Banking System. It is implemented on an independent platform and is deployed, according to Temenos, as a Message Bean on standard JEE application servers. It contains web service and Odata interfaces to external software components and also offers a user interface presumably used by bank employees at the counter and in the back office. Furthermore, this architecture offers design tools for model-driven development and change deployment, which means that it also supports model driven development tools. The T24 component contains all modules from the Front Office to the Back Office and is complemented with (likely subsequently added) further modules like the T24 CRM module, a payment suite and a data source module. The basic task of the data source module is to support the import and export, the analysis and the procession of data. A Business Intelligence component runs in parallel to the three areas Front Office, Middle Office and Back Office, which allows the calculation of customized key performance indicators out of the data base.

Temenos is technologically considered to be a heterogeneous system. The core is likely to large extent implemented in Java, which means that it contains components which are written in plain Java and some which are written using J2EE. SVN and maven is used for code versioning and dependency management. And as an application server either Jboss, WebSphere, GlassFish, the Apache Tomcat Server and in some circumstances WebLogic instances are used. The data storage is realized with MS SQL Servers and Oracle Servers, which are accessed through PL/SQL scripts and object relational mapping frameworks like Hibernate. In addition to the previously mentioned databases, the Temenos CBS also relies on Neo 4J databases, although it should be mentioned that they are not relational, but graph based.

In general, Temenos works to a large extent with Java and technologies which rely heavily on Java. However Temenos also partially works with .net/C#. For the clients, Temenos uses JavaS-cript HTML5, CSS3, Jquery and Ajax and regarding the Server infrastructure, Windows Server Operating Systems as well as Linux and Unix based operating systems are used for deployment. After summarizing the previously outlined components and technologies, Temenos is likely to have an architecture which is depicted in Illustration 10.

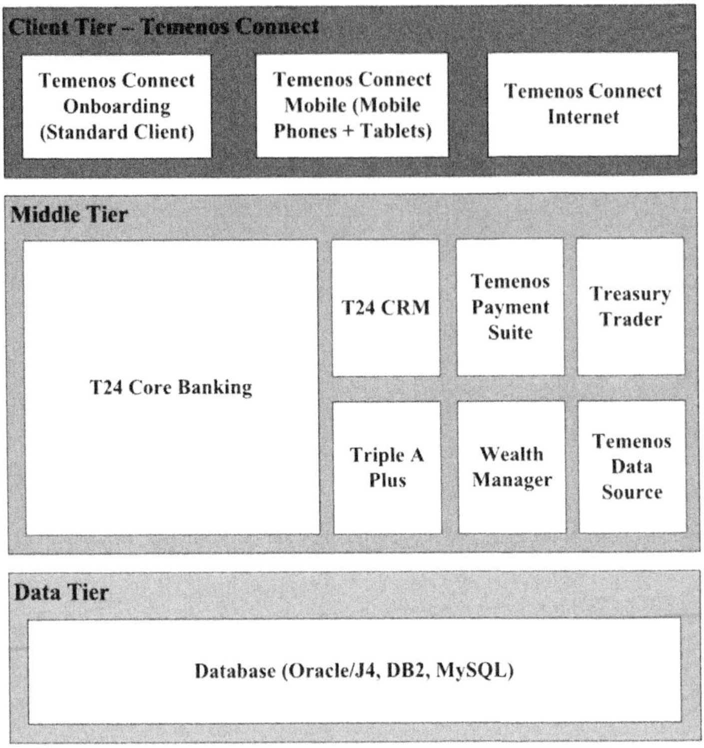

Illustration 10: The prospected Overall Architecture of Temenos [82]

On the basis of this architecture it is apparent that the modules of Temenos were likely developed around the T24 Core Banking Framework. The T24 core module can be deployed on different servers with different operating systems (Linux, AIX, HP-UX, Solaris, NT, Windows) due to its platform independence. The User Interface connection is realized through a web server which interacts with the T24 application server via TCP/IP socket interfaces. For the various functions in the presentation layer, the Temenos Core Banking System utilizes several different technologies.

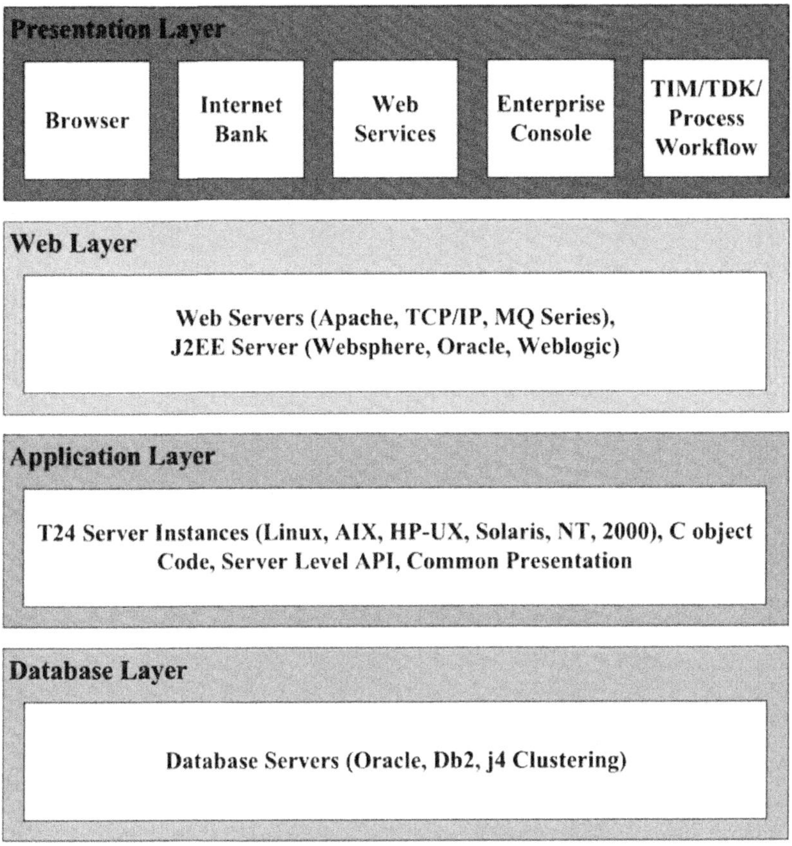

Illustration 11: The Deployment View of Temenos [82]

The T24 application server is divided into five components (Retail Banking, Private Banking, Treasury Banking, Corporate Banking and General Banking), that are in turn subdivided into further functional modules.

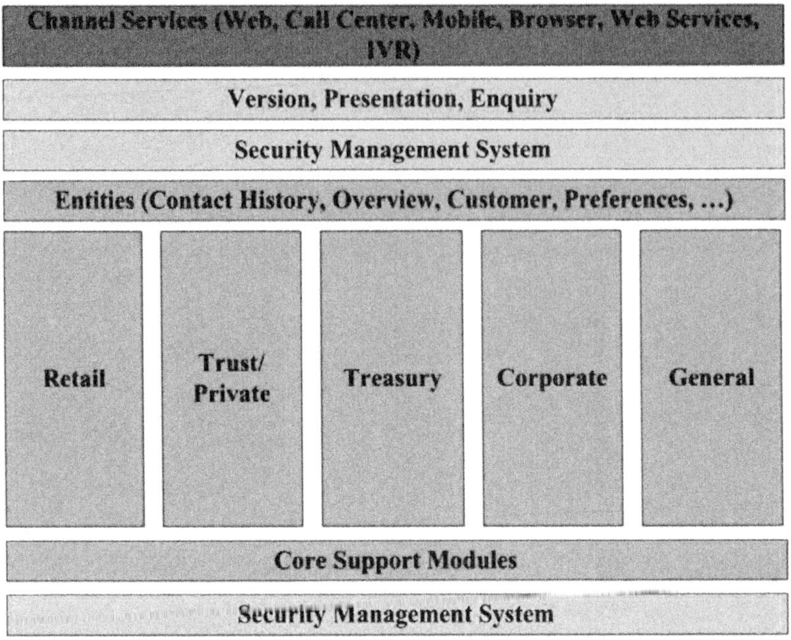

Illustration 12: Functional Overview of the T24 Core Module [82]

4.3.4 Oracle Flexcube

Oracle Flexcube [89] was initially developed in the mid-1990s by a company called CITIL in its development center in Bangalore. The company (later renamed to i-flex Solutions and afterwards - in 2008 - to Oracle Financial Services Software) was originally founded as part of the CITI-BANK group and was taken over by Oracle in August 2005. Oracle Financial Services Software (OFSS) offers a range of products, which cover the needs of the financial branch as well as other divisions. One of these products is the Flexcube Universal Banking Suite which is currently used by more than 600 customers in more than 140 countries and designed for rather large banks that operate on an international and multilanguage level. Functionally it is divided into the following modules, each of which may be individually acquired by a customer:

- Core Banking
- Universal Banking
- Investor Servicing
- Private Banking
- Lending and Leasing

- Islamic Banking
- Direct Banking- Internet, Mobile, SMS and WAP
- Messaging Hub
- Remit
- Enterprise Limits and Collateral Management

In terms of its architecture, it has a four-layer architecture, whereas its functionality is modularized in a service oriented topology.

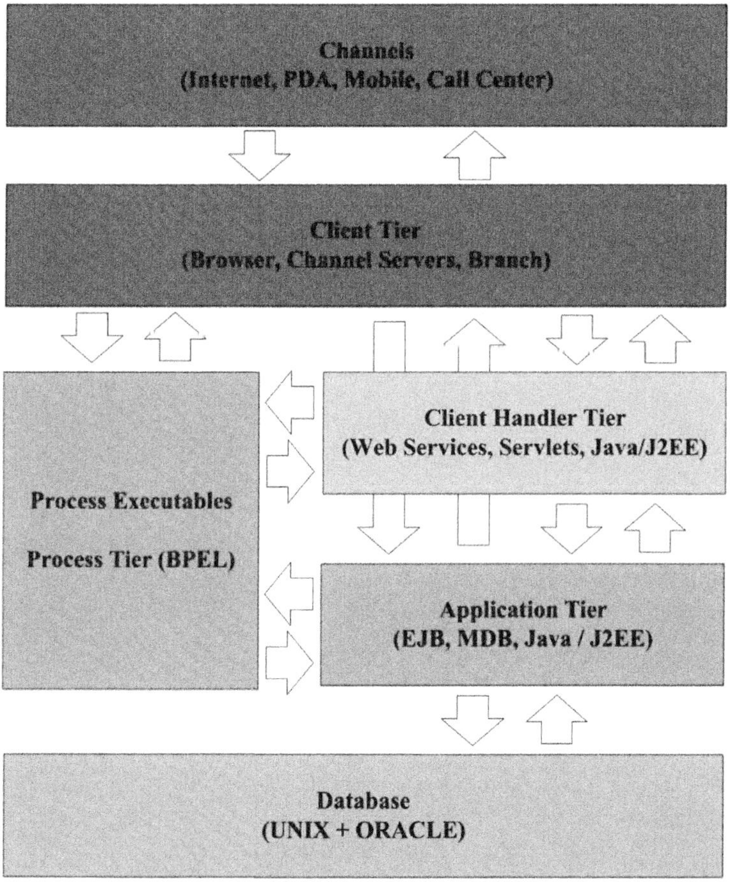

Illustration 13: The Layered Architecture of Flexcube [89]

The database tier consists mainly of a relational database, with particular emphasis being put on Oracle 11g by Flexcube. The database itself is topologically divided into three types of tables;

maintenance tables, internal tables and temporary work tables. The maintenance tables are accessed from the front-end, and may be indirectly manipulated by the user through the application (e.g. through entering information into a form and submitting it to the server). Internal tables are only manipulated through automated data processing by front-end or back-end program units. And the temporary tables are used by program routines to intermittently store the data needed to achieve their purpose. The data is deleted after the routine has finished its given task. Aside from the database, this tier also contains business logic in the form of PL/SQL scripts which are executed via services of the database and therefore yield a quick runtime as there is no intermediate component between them and the database. Between the database layer and the application layer is a middleware integration module which handles module specific services. It is responsible for the communication with the application layer, and the communication is conducted via JDBC and XML. According to its development overview guide the Application and Integration Tier is mainly based on Java related technologies and houses the business logic itself in the form of 95 functional modules. Additionally, it is also responsible for the interaction of Flexcube functionality with its own clients-, as well as external components. Furthermore, it provides message handling as well as session and transaction management. The transaction management is realized through EJB and MDB (Enterprise- and message driven Java Beans) and communicates with the handlers and the session management through XML and Java APIs. These in turn communicate with respective clients, e.g. the HTTP Handler interacts with the with HTTP clients via XML and HTTP while the Web services handler uses XML / SOAP in order to send and receive messages from required Web Service based clients.

On top of the Application and Integration Tier is the Process Tier which provides the ability to create processes, that work in parallel to the Application itself. They can be implemented as Oracle BPEL processes (Business Process Execution Language) and are maintained through a respective BPEL process manager. Later on in the process they may be included in the user interface framework as tasks. The process manager is connected to the transaction management and may interact with web service based clients and the client browser through their respective handlers, depending on the demands of the processes which are executed on it.

The fourth tier is the user interface layer containing a browser based native Flexcube client. XML is used in order to communicate with the application (client handler) and is configurable as well as multilingual. Dedicated channel servers exist in addition to the client which are used for auxiliary (external) user interface channels like mobile clients, or online banking which are Web Service based.

The functional architecture of Flexcube is highly based on its Integration Layer which provides internal as well as external services via a client to the user. Internally, Flexcube is divided into two business modules, and three service groups, which in turn consist of various subservices each covering an aspect of its overall functionality. The following graph shows an overview over Flexcube's functional topology.

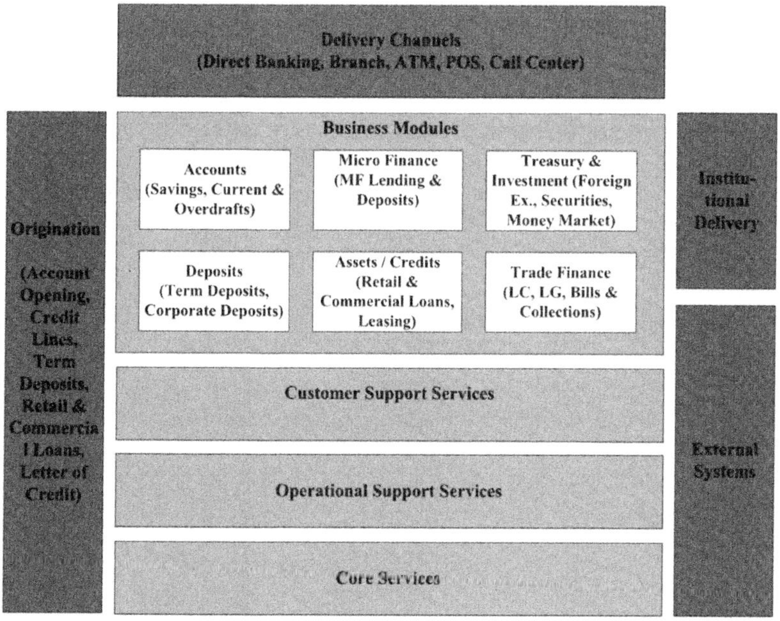

Illustration 14: The Functional Topology of Flexcube [89]

In terms of technologies and programming languages, Flexcube uses state-of-the-art technologies which generally utilize Java as the source programming language. The backend tier of this architecture utilizes SQL, PL/SQL and Java in its Core Version, whereas the application layer uses J2EE related technologies such as EJB, MDB, Servlets, JNDI, JDBC, JSB and JMS, as well as BPEL as the language for the specification of customized processes. On the Frontend, XHTML, Java Script, DOM and CSS are used.

Regarding deployment, Flexcube can also be deployed on large infrastructures as it is intended to run in datacentres, with server clusters on the database side as well as the application server side. It supports two deployment modes, namely a centralized approach and a decentralized one. In the centralized approach, the application and the database are hosted in one virtual cloud based data centre and every branch of a customer bank interacts with the CBS through accessing that datacentre. In the decentralized approach, a centralized database in a host datacentre still exists, but additionally each branch is given the freedom to use the local branch databases as well. This is especially necessary in case certain branches are obliged to physically host certain data within a country's borders due to national laws of their respective country of operation. As already shown, Flexcube physically separates its data from the application by using dedicated database servers which are organised in so called 'load balanced eXecutive high-availability clusters' in order to prevent single points of failures. The same principle applies to the application servers, which are also organized into load balanced clusters and are both dynamically as well as logically partitioned. The physical disks behind the clusters are protected against disk failure through RAID 1+0 and the entire system is also mirrored in a disaster recovery (DR) site where the data of the production site is constantly replicated.

4.3.5 Finacle

Finacle [90] was first released in 1999 by the Indian company Infosys and is now used by banks in more than hundred countries. Like Flexcube, its target group are major banks, working on international levels and according to its web presence it is used by 16,5% of the world's banks. In 2015 it was taken over by EdgeVerve (also an Indian subcompany of InfoSys). Overall it can be said that the main portion of its customers are located in south-east Asia and Africa. Functionally, it is a suite of different products, whereas the following are the main ones:

- Core Banking
- Universal Banking
- CRM
- Treasury as well as Wealth Management
- Direct- and Mobile Banking
- Islamic Banking
- Payments
- E-Banking
- Besides to that there exist several minor products like a Youth Banking Solutions, Small Finance Bank Solutions or Alerts and Analytics Solutions.

In addition to its Core functionality, Finacle also utilizes a number of different frameworks and support services with the aim to increase the maintainability as well as the adaptability of the CBS as a whole. A batch framework for the asynchronous event, or time triggered execution of batch jobs is an example of this. Aside from that, they also include an identity access management system in order to give their customers the opportunity to control authentication as well as authorization of the internal (bank clerks) and external (bank customers) user groups. As the availability of a CBS is usually a critical attribute to a bank, internal application monitoring procedures are also implemented with the purpose to ensure the CBS' health while it is operating. Finacle also contains tools to address the adaptability requirements of the customers which enable banks to add custom functionalities to their respective installations. These functionalities include scripting frameworks, interfaces to BPM tools, reporting engines, internal document management functionality and tools for code customization. On the end user side, Finacle's infrastructural services are comprised of functions such as Single Sign On, Signature Verification and Customer Information Files.

From a technological perspective, Finacle relies heavily on Java- and Java related technologies, whereas its Core functions are implemented in C/C++. Its technical architecture is roughly outlined in Illustration 15.

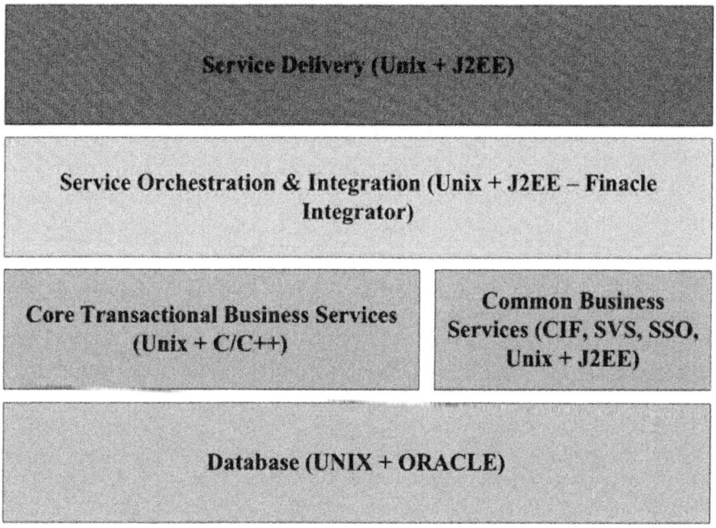

Illustration 15: The layered Architecture of Finacle [90]

According to its technology architecture, Finacle is overall deployed on a Unix Operating System and covers four horizontal layers, ranging from data management (Oracle Database) to a J2EE based frontend. As outlined above, the Core Transactional Business Services are encompassed by Common Business Services which are not directly Core Banking functions but deliver common infrastructural and business services. On top of Finacle's Core and Common Services lies an integration layer which is responsible for the intercommunication between the logic and clients as well as third party components via XML and J2EE related interfaces like web services, JMS (Java Messaging System) or EJB (Enterprise Java Beans). The service delivery layer is situated above the interface layer and essentially plays the role of the client layer. It is also implemented in J2EE technologies and contains several clients, including a mobile banking as well as an e-banking client, which are deployed via web sphere servers and are intended for the customer user group. The bank clerk interface consists of a rich client which is modularized depending on the purchased functionality. In addition to the clients, further communication channels have been considered for the customers, such as SMS or E-Mail. Aside from that, Finacle also offers communication channels in order to communicate with external components such as hardware, like ATMs or self-service terminals.

In terms of functional organization, Finacle is a host based system and consists out of numerous components, each of which is a major business module within the entire service landscape. These business modules are in turn separated into various layers and divided into functional groups and subgroups. Each subgroup (as a service) communicates over the so called Finacle Solution Bus (a CBS wide communication framework) with other subgroups. For the purpose of data transactions, the Solution Bus internally utilizes different technological channels such as JMS, Java based message queues as well as SOAP Web Services and TCP/IP Socket communications. The Solution Bus is not only responsible for the service-to-service communication, but also for the communication from the backend to the front-end. Architecturally, it encapsulates the interface and client layer from the Host which contains the core business logic and the connection to the database. Illustration 16 shows a rough architecture of Finacle.

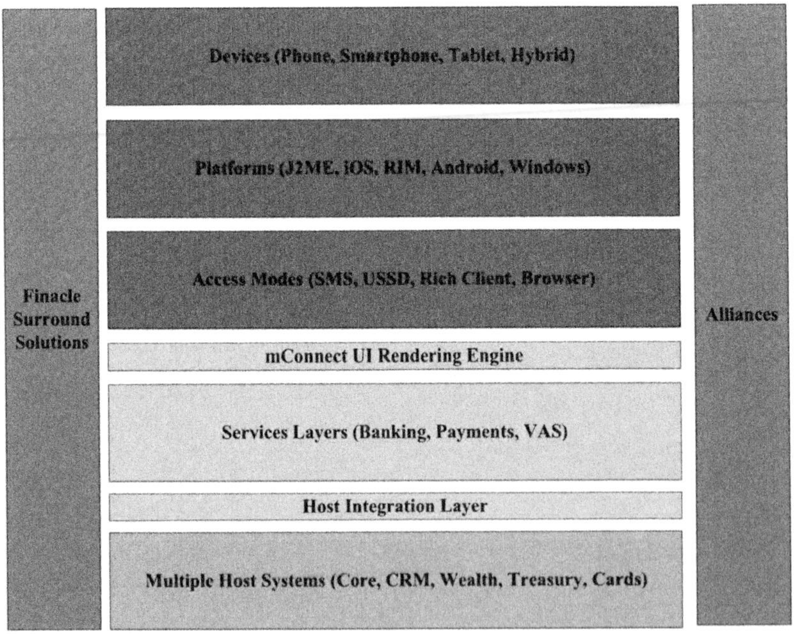

Illustration 16: The Functional Architecture of Finacle [90]

4.4 Analysis of existing CBS

In this section, first the weakpoints as well as the strongpoints of each previously outlined CBS architectures will be discussed and subsequentially, they will be compared according to a set of criteria.

4.4.1 Weakpoints vs. Strongpoints

4.4.1.1 Avaloq

A strongpoint of Avaloq is its use of a Model Driven Development Approach in order to modernize its code step by step. That means old source code is used as a basis for generating new business objects. Model Driven Development has high initial costs but it proves profitable in the long run. Furthermore, Avaloq also developed its own IDE (integrated development environment), which enables customers to adapt their local Avaloq deployment according to their own requirements and needs. The IDE is based on Eclipse and is enriched through self-developed plugins. With the help of the IDE, customers can define their own business processes in BPMN notation, which are then automatically transformed into Source code. The advantage of this idea is, that customers are included into in the development process and the functional flexibility of Avaloq is decisively increased. For instance, business objects, which were initially developed by the vendor may be used by the customer bank in a completely different context. Another benefit is that customers do not need to have sophisticated programming skills since the functionality is defined on a higher and abstracted level in BPMN.

In contrast to that, one of Avaloq's weak points is its use of PL/SQL in order to interact with its database. PL/SQL is a comparably old Oracle technology that was introduced in 1991 and consequently is mainly usable for Oracle databases. Other DBMS (database management system) vendors keep their systems compatible to PL/SQL however, they are always one step behind the innovations of Oracle. Furthermore, PL/SQL is not object oriented but procedural, which in turn means that Avaloq is not object oriented in its entirety. Additionally, PL/SQL obstructs a technological change to a different DBMS and hence increases the technological dependency of Avaloq towards Oracle. Another drawback is, that Avaloq implemented its core logic partially in C# and in parts in Java. This duality in terms of programming languages is not ideal, as it hampers the communication within the middle tier and creates overhead in general. Nevertheless, it is an indicator for the transformation process, which is currently ongoing within the Avaloq framework. Except from that, the CBS is not platform independent which is a technological implication of the source code written in C#.

4.4.1.2 Finnova

An architectural advantage of Finnova's Core Banking System is that is uses a Kernel in order to centrally control and steer functional workflows. The basic concept behind that approach offers an enormous amount of opportunities and is open to future changes. Also similar to Avaloq, Finnova uses a development kit, which enables customers to adapt their specific Finnova deployment fitting to their own requirements. According to public sources, the Finnova development kit does not seem as being on the same level of sophistication as the one Avaloq offers, since the BPMN component seems to be missing and therefore customers must possess programming skills. But nevertheless it offers facilities for individual adaptions including their resulting advantages. However, much like Avaloq, Finnova uses PL/SQL in order to communicate with its database. This implies the same problems in terms of object orientation and platform dependence.

4.4.1.3 Temenos

Temenos tries to remain as technologically flexible as possible by utilizing different database technologies, which are not only restricted to Oracle. Using this principle, it remains independent from Oracle and may work with different database technologies. Besides to that, Temenos also uses a framework called Connect UXP, enabling the vendor to create new HTML 5 based clients rapidly. These clients can communicate with the Temenos application server, but are also compatible with different applications.

On the other side a drawback of Temenos is its T24 core. Instead of redesigning the T24 core itself, Temenos began to create further applications around the T24 Banking Framework. That means that the T24 core module, in all probability, is based on old technologies which will need to be modernized in the longer term. Except from that, in public sources as well as in user manuals, there was information available about the architectural conception around the T24 core module. However, despite extensive recherché, there were no specific information supplied about the architecture within the T24 core module. This indicates, that the vendor might try to hide the core architecture from public. In combination with the fact that the T24 core module is technologically heterogeneous, this implies that the T24 core module is based on old, outgrown source code.

4.4.1.4 Oracle Flexcube

Flexcube is, compared to other CBS, a rather new Core Banking System, which relies on state of the art technologies. Its Core language is Java and its functionalities are all based on technologies which are related to Java. Hence, its technology stack is rather homogeneous, as the base technology is mainly Java. The application is platform independent as it is encapsulated into a Java Virtual Machine. Another architectural advantage is that it utilizes a kernel based process tier, which allows the creation of centrally governed business processes. These business processes are also a gateway for customer side customization. Furthermore, Flexcube also uses a decentralized data storing approach, which enables customers to store parts of data in a central datacenter as well as in local branches. This implies great flexibility in terms of data storage, but may also imply performance issues due to necessary data transfers.

However, since Flexcube is an Oracle Product, it is heavily bound to oracle technologies, especially through the use of Oracle databases and PL/SQL. This reduces its technological flexibility slightly. And also in Flexcube the business logic is implemented in PL/SQL scripts. The proximity to the database on the one hand increases performance, but on the other hand the framework is bound to PL/SQL as a technology and respectively difficult to migrate. Furthermore, Flexcube is not object oriented due to the use of PL/SQL.

4.4.1.5 Finacle

Finacle was developed from scratch and hence adopts modern software engineering standards. Additionally, it learned from other CBS systems and keeps a focus on maintainability and adaptability in terms of its architecture, which is definitely an advantage. It also offers its customers the facility to extend its framework by custom code, which increases its adaptability and involves the customer in the development process. It does so by providing scripting frameworks a BPM tool and customer side reporting engines. In addition, compared to other CBS, its technology stack is rather state of the art as the main programming languages are Java as well as C and C++. And another strongpoint is Finacle's use of a service bus, which standardizes internal communication and makes the entire framework more integrable towards new components.

But on the other side, Finacle uses two different main programming languages, which reduces its maintainability and also removes its platform independence.

4.4.2 Comparison and Resume

In the context of modernization, it does not make sense to compare or rank the previously discussed Core Banking examples directly against each other as CBS are generally too heterogeneous and their different objectives and customer groups are too varied. But it is a valid approach to select a number of criteria which are related to architectural modernization in the context of Core Banking Systems and to choose the strongpoints from each of the previous examples in order to evaluate them [62, 63]. The selected criteria are the following:

- Technological Flexibility – is the flexibility with which a technology within the CBS' technology stack may be exchanged by another.
- Technological Heterogeneity – is the number of technologies, which are required to provide a certain functionality.

- Modularization - The extent to which the entire framework is divided into functional modules, which in turn affects the interchangeability of certain functions.
- Scalability - The ability of the framework to adapt to changing numbers of users (e.g. through a constantly growing number of users) on a platform level as well as a functional level.
- Modifiability - The ability to change existing functional components.
- Adaptability – The ability to customize existing functional components to the specifications of a customer bank.

In general, newer CBS have less technological and architectural debts, in the form of outdated core components, which need to be reconditioned. Furthermore, their advantage is that they have the chance to learn from already existing CBS and to address their challenges from an architectural perspective in a early stage. While Temenons or Finnova consist partially of outdated components, written in technologies from the 1970s and 1980s, younger CBS such as Flexcube or Finacle had the chance and the resources to create a comparably new Core Banking framework from scratch, where architectural sustainability had been greatly emphasized. This is further reflected in the fact that the choice of programming languages is more state of the art and the surrounding technologies are usually related to these programming languages. Also the data model is more integrated and designed in a way that enables comparably easy modifications in the future. In terms of technological flexibility, Temenos tried to remain independent from any specific database vendor through creating different ways to attach a database to its solution, although Oracle seems to be the main database technology provider in that matter. Regarding technological heterogeneity, the more technologies a CBS uses, the more complex it is to modernize it. Hence, it is recommendable to use one main programming language and to attempt to utilize technologies which are related or based on that language as opposed to technologies based on other languages. Although technologically tightly bound to Oracle, Flexcube has a decisive advantage as it is mainly implemented in Java and related state of the art technologies. By doing so it also harnesses all advantages which come with Java including platform independence, a large number of support and related technologies which is also induced by the extensive market share of Java as a technology. And due to the global distribution of Java, respective tool support for the migration frameworks has been developed. In connection with modularization, all of the examined CBS use a layer based topology, which allows the relatively easy replacement of certain layers, with the front client usually being the most frequently exchanged component. Within the application layer, CBS often either use a component based modularization approach (e.g. Flexcube) or a process based approach (compare to Finnova). Since processes are usually more interconnected with other processes and components, they are considered to be harder to replace. Therefore, modularization on a service based approach might be a better option for layered grouping. Flexcube utilizes this

approach by dividing its functionality into business modules, which are in turn divided into service groups and subservices. These services are then invoked by one another in order to form a business process.
In terms of scalability, all vendors definitely faced the challenge that one application server and one database server might not be enough to cope with the load of constant employee and customer transactions. Hence, all vendors support a clustering mechanism which disperses the user load over several application server and database server instances. However, in this regard Flexcube has a more sophisticated approach compared to others as it is already designed to work from a cloud. Therefore, it is capable of operating in a private or hybrid cloud which is massively scalable and currently one of the main technological concepts in industrial computing. Also the fact, that it supports dispersed databases is an advantage for scalability. The modifiability of a CBS depends on both its technology stack and modularization, as well as its internal communication. The more standardized an internal communication framework is, the easier it is to replace certain functionality assuming that it is properly delimited from other functions. In that regard Finacle has an architectural advantage through the use of its service bus. It works as a standard interface from one service to another and abstracts the code as well as the technology in which the logic behind an interface is implemented. Hence, if the logic behind the connected interfaces is properly separated (e.g. in the form of self-contained modules or services), then it is comparably simple to replace it through another component, which may perform the same task in a different way and which may be even written in a different language. Finally, in terms of adaptability, all of the previously described CBS offer frameworks which enable the customer to customize their local CBS deployment. However, Avaloq presents a particularly straightforward solution by equipping the customer with a plugin enriched Eclipse distribution. This customized workbench does not require sophisticated programming skills from the customer but enables them to adapt or add functionality according to the model based coding standards of Avaloq.

4.5 Exemplary Architecture of a CBS

The architecture which is described in this chapter is a self-developed exemplary illustration of a CBS architecture which could exist in reality and shall serve as an example for a modernization in the following chapters.
In this scenario, the CBS is a grown system, which was developed over the course of several decades for rather small regionally operating banks. In the beginning, it was only focused on Retail banks and extended its functionality step by step towards Private and Investment banking as it gained several customers in that field over time. In order to quickly create functional value for its customers and due to a lack of personnel, its vendor decided on several occasions to buy

submodules from other specialized vendors and to integrate them into its framework. Architecturally it is roughly split up into four layers where the bottom layer is a data tier, consisting out of three different databases, an application tier an interface tier and a client tier. The application tier contains a module for core banking as well as components for related functionality, a CRM module and a trading module. The client layer is composed out of a rich client which has to be installed on a target platform and an online banking application.

4.5.1 Functional Overview

In terms of its functionality, the CBS is split up into the following topological branches:

- Core banking: Covering electronic funds transfer, account current, private- and corporate loans and card management.
- CRM: Covering customer management, customer core data, customer scoring, customer account management, and document management.
- Private/investment banking: Consisting out of asset management, order management/processing, portfolio management, customer risk management, market data/modelling, and ALM (asset liability management).
- Support component: Containing modules for internal accounting and balancing, controlling, internal risk management, regulatory reporting and internal revision.

The CBS has two clients. The first one is intended for the bank's clerks and is to be installed locally on each user workplace. The second client is a web based client, serving for online banking purposes of the bank's customers and shall give them the opportunity to maintain their accounts online, including the issue of online transactions. In its functionality the online banking client realizes the following features:

- Access to Giro- and savings accounts as well as their transaction histories.
- Maintenance of bank- and credit cards.
- Issuing of one time transactions as well as the creation and maintenance of standing orders.
- Processing requests of account statements.
- Access to personal loans including their transaction histories.

4.5.2 Functional Architecture

Illustration 17 shows a rough overview of the CBS and its conceptual architecture.

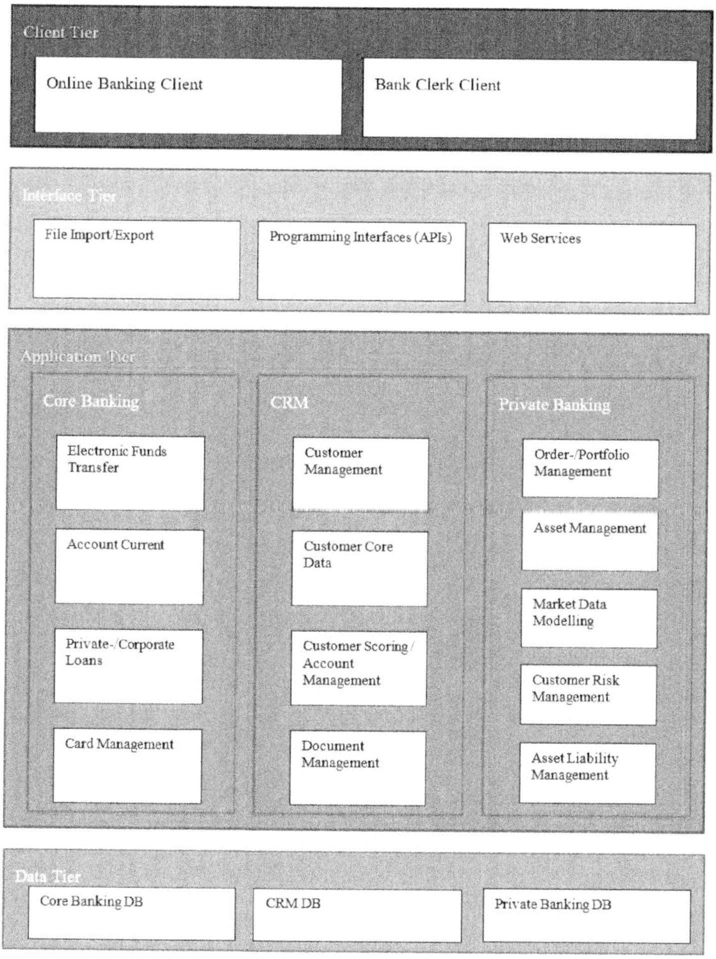

Illustration 17: The Functional Architecture of the outlined CBS

4.5.2.1 Data Tier

In terms of the infrastructure the CBS runs on two different Linux servers with one serving as a database server for the data tier and the other one as an application server for the application tier. The CBS is architecturally split up into several modules which were appended over time during the CBS' development. The CRM module and the private and investment banking modules were acquired through a commercial acquisition of their vendors and integrated into the existing CBS solution.

As a result of the additions to the architecture, the data tier consists out of three separated databases, which do not directly interact with each other and only cooperate with their counterparts via the application tier. The core banking (CB) support database houses the data which is processed by the Support and Core Banking modules within the application layer. It has its own data scheme and contains account data, transaction records and histories, primanotas, data from account balances and controlling data which is processed within the support functionality. The database is designed using automatically incremented IDs within each table but does not use foreign keys in order to prevent data inconsistencies. Technologically, it is a MySQL database [97], which already succeeds a previous database technology. The second database is a postgres database [98] which houses the CRM data of the Core Banking System. That means, its main data entities are customers and persons with their core data as well as their connections to each other and their interactions with the respective bank. In contrast to the first DB, foreign keys and field constraints are used freely in this database. The third database covers the private and investment banking functionality, with the information being stored consisting mainly of security paper transaction data, orders, market data and risk related data. It is realized in form of an Oracle DB [99] and makes extensive use of stored procedures, functions and triggers.

4.5.2.2 Application Tier

The following illustration depicts the overall structure of the CBS on the application server.

```
/app
  | - /card       (card management)
  | - /cb         (core banking)
  | - /crm        (customer relation management)
  | - /eft        (electronic funds transfer)
  | - /pb         (private banking)
  | - /support
  | - ...
```

Each of the modules contains its own software project with the encompassing compilation frameworks, programs, support libraries, global constants and specific preferences.

The main module (and also the oldest) among them is the Core Banking module, which was initially designed to run on an IBM AS400 [100] and was therefore written in Report Code Generator (RPG) II and III code [101] and migrated to RPG IV code over time. It consists out of a number of RPG programs which may interact with each other and call each other during their runtime. They are compiled via a Unix based Lattice-RPG compiler [102] to artefacts which are then delivered using hotfixes to customers. Internally the Core Banking module is split up into sub modules where each submodule is a simple folder, containing its relevant RPG programs. If a user calls a certain functionality from the rich client, it takes input values from the user interface and inserts them as input parameters into a data structure which is afterwards sent to the server in the form of a TCP/IP request [103]. In addition to the appropriate parameters, the data structure also contains a transaction code which enables the server to identify and call the needed RPG program. As soon as the appropriate program creates relevant output for the user it is packed again into a data structure and sent to the rich client as a response to the TCP request. During its runtime the RPG program may also interact with the Core Banking database through SQL statements [104] that are directly embedded in its source code. The values are then slotted through RPG variables and transformed into valid SQL statements through an RPG SQL pre-processor. The communication with the database happens through a Java based JDBC driver [105], which conveys the statement to the MySQL DB and returns its result to the program. Aside from the Core Banking module, the Support component is also written in RPG, as it was developed over time in parallel to the CB part. It is technologically equally designed as the CB functionality and therefore shares its common resources (libraries, constants, global variables, etc.) with the CB module, nevertheless its code is situated in its own working folder.

The CRM module was acquired by taking over its vendor and integrating it into the existing CBS framework. It is based on Java and uses its own CRM database and is also a grown system but slightly younger than the CB component, which implies that it is based on newer / more recent Java related technologies. In contrast to the procedural programming style of RPG, this component is object oriented and uses objects which are reflected as entities in the database. Furthermore, it is internally split according to the MVC pattern (see section 3.2.3.3.5) with interfaces between the persistence functions and business logic and also interfaces between the business logic and the client. The Support component uses its own build management tool (Apache ANT [106]), in order to generate binaries out of the source code, and utilizes logging tools as well as an object-relational (OR) mapper framework [107].

The private banking component is written in plain C and interacts with its own Oracle database via PL/SQL [108]. Similar to the Core Banking component, it consists out of a number of individual programs which may be invoked separately through internal identification codes. The CRM and the private banking components are both deployed on a Unix machine but hosted on different application servers in order to be kept available to the clients. Furthermore, the programming paradigm of the private banking component is not object oriented but instead procedural and the resulting executable functions are compiled via makefiles [109]. The communication between the three layers happens on the one side through an internal communication toolkit, which serves on the one hand as an adapter between the main components and on the other hand as a messaging system comparable to an Enterprise Service Bus [110]. The internal communication toolkit was developed out of the need to integrate the three components with each other and is extended on demand. CRM, private banking and core banking share the trait that they all are hosted on the same Unix system [111], which means that the development environment as well as any test- and production environments are usually located on one dedicated server.

4.5.2.3 Interface Tier

The main task of the interface tier is to manage the data transfer from the application layer to the clients and third party applications via defined interfaces. Likewise, it consists out of different interfaces which are categorized in three groups. The first group is a file import- and export mechanism which communicates with other stakeholders through text files that are stored and fetched from defined network locations within the bank's IT infrastructure. The text files may either be plain text files containing data records, or semi-structured on the basis of XML [112]. The text files are exported and imported through time or event triggered jobs (batch jobs) and serve mainly to realize secured payment data transfer as well as data transfer to other banks. The file export mechanism encapsulates the automated creation of files at defined locations including content which is formatted according to given constraints. These constraints include line lengths, maximum amounts of lines, character encoding and file metadata. On the import side, data needs to be parsed from a given file and interpreted, which involves error handling as well.
The second group is based on Java implemented APIs and interfaces which allow third parties and clients direct and standardized access to the application tier's functionality. The APIs were implemented over time, depending on requirements of the CBS user banks and their need to integrate the CBS into their respective IT infrastructure. The APIs main task is to abstract the application server from the outside so that no direct conversion from the CRM component to the interface layer is necessary, as the implementing language is the same. The interaction between the private banking tower (written in C [113]) as well as the Core Banking tower (RPG code) and the APIs is realized through the use of JNI (Java Native Interfaces [114]). They enable Java implemented interfaces which cover functions implemented in both languages.
The third group is based on SOAP Web Services with the main purpose of communicating with the client layer of the CBS. Specifically, the Web Services are based on a SOAP envelope [115] which encapsulates XML content in its body and is transferred to and from the clients via HTTP [116].

4.5.2.4 Client Tier

As depicted in Illustration 17, the client layer consists out of two different clients where one is intended for the bank's internal staff, and the other one is a web based online banking client with the purpose of enabling end customer access to their accounts.

4.5.2.4.1 Online Banking Client

The online banking client interacts with the application server through web services and is based on JavaScript [117] and AngularJS [118]. Users access it from a browser via an SSL [119] encrypted HTTPS session and need to login in by providing their customer number and a password. They are then redirected to an overview page from where they can execute use cases, belonging to the respective banking products, which were previously obtained from the bank. To them belong the inspection of personal accounts, loans, credit cards. But also the issuing of standing orders, as well as any kind of payment transactions are encompassed by these use cases.
In the course of these use cases the online banking client issues read or write requests to the application. For instance, if a user intends to issue a money transaction, the online banking client first needs to fetch the required data from the application server and the database at the backend. The data then needs to be presented to the user in an appropriate form so that they are able to fill in the respective data and submit the order. The order must be transferred to the application server, where it will be checked against any constraints (e.g. account limits, or the account balance), and processed accordingly. Next, the resulting data needs to be persisted in the database and the user needs to be informed with a response about the success, or failure of their transaction. From a physical perspective, the online banking client is deployed on an Apache Tomcat server [120], which is in turn installed on the application server.

4.5.2.4.2 Internal Client

The internal client is intended for the bank's staff and is an installed Java based rich client application. It communicates with the Interface Tier through the invocation of APIs and the File Import- and export mechanism, as bank clerks need to be able to store files within the CBS (e.g. scanned loan or account opening contracts). The basic communication mechanism is in principle the same as the online banking client, with the difference that the APIs are invoked through Java RMI [121] and that input validation is already conducted within the client instead of the application. From a functional perspective, a bank clerk needs to authenticate before being able to access the data of his customer stock and transform it through different use cases. The bank clerk's privileges are restricted to a certain set of customers which are assigned to him. Accordingly he may only execute actions on them and their accounts to the extent which he is entitled according to his role within the bank. Additionally, a number of transactions (e.g. the approval of large amount money transactions with regard to anti money laundering regulations) need to be verified through another person according to the 4-eye principle. Some of the main use cases are the creation of new accounts for new customers as well as their maintenance in regard to account conditions, account limits or account closure. Furthermore, transactions in connection to loans as well as cash desk operations are also common in the day-to-day business of a bank clerk.

4.5.2.5 Internal Communication

As already mentioned, the internal communication of the application server is realized through a dual purpose self-developed communication toolkit. First, it acts as an adapter in order to integrate different functions of the CBS with each other and to give them the ability to interact. Second, it works as a messaging system through exchanging triggered messages from one component to another one. The communication toolkit is a rudimentary proprietary development in order to integrate the Core Banking tower with the CRM private banking tower and the CRM module. Within each tower, the functional modules and programs mainly interact through direct invocations of a target application, which then works in its own instance depending on how often it was invoked. Hence, there is no common process management which handles running threads, or conducts consistent error handling in case an application fails during a transaction or gets stuck.

The communication toolkit itself works on the basis of remote procedure calls, where each service is registered in a broker service with a defined interface that is translated into a self-designed protocol. The protocol consists out of a header containing meta and address data as well as a data packet. The header is in principle a text array with a number of standardized fields, including the source and the target service as defined in the broker service, the size of the following data packet, a sequence number, the total number of packets for the entire message and a checksum in order to verify the integrity of the packet. The data packet is also a plain buffer of a standardized size and each message consists of at least one data packet. The adapters are used in converting a message from a native function to the protocol format and vice versa and were written over time in the programming languages of the three towers, depending on where they were needed. They are also responsible for splitting a message into packages for sending and assembling received packets to a single data message.

The messaging framework itself is written in C and has no central communication controlling instance. Instead, a message transmission is managed and verified by the receiving service with the help of a message queue. Within the queue, packets are assembled into a message and are ranked for further processing. The queue also prevents race conditions in the case that packages from several senders are received at the same time. Each package is also verified with the help of the delivered checksum and if a package is missing or damaged, the receiver notifies the sender, in order to initiate a resending of the affected package.

4.5.3 Logical Architecture

The logical architecture focuses on functional aspects of a CBS and contains a logical structure without constraining the CBS to a specific technology.

4.5.3.1 Functional View

From a logical perspective the CBS is process oriented with the central processes being bound to one of the three towers. That means, if a user wants to run a certain use case, input data must be transmitted via one of the clients to the CBS and triggers the execution of a program. That program begins to transform the input data (in parts with the help of data from the database) and, if required, invokes other programs as well. These programs then fulfil their function, transform the data which is required in the course of the process and persist it in their respective database. Once the process reaches its end the invoking program is informed about the result of their actions and the main program then returns the resulting data (or result of the process) to the client, which is depicted to the user. So logically and functionally the CBS is divided into a number of programs that are grouped together in functional modules. These programs are then used as building blocks in order to realize business processes (use cases), which in the end fulfil the needs of the user. However, the CBS is divided into three self-developed or bought functional realms which are only integrated as needed, with inter-tower communication occuring only where needed.

4.5.3.2 User View and Logical Security

The users of the CBS are divided into two main groups; service users and natural users. On the one hand service users are always anonymous and are either used for automated jobs, which are either time or event triggered, or for the interaction with third party systems. On the other hand, personalized users are split into four user groups; internal bank staff, end customers, administrators and the bank's internal revision. These four user groups are disjunctive, which means that an administrator, bank clerk or revisor can never be a bank customer with the same account. In the situation where they are also a customer as well, they are provided with a separate account. All user and service accounts are subject to a common authorization repository, where the privileges of each account are stored. The authorization system is both role and group based, which means that a user may belong to a certain group containing a number of roles with the authorization to execute a defined set of actions. Administrators and revisors have no direct access to the clients via their logins and are hence not allowed to conduct business logic transactions which clerks or customers may perform. However, they may access the CBS infrastructure directly through respective frameworks (e.g. database clients, or direct server access). In contrast to them, the access of bank clerks to the internal client of the CBS is single-sign-on (SSO) integrated with their workplace accounts that allow the execution of a privilege restricted set of use cases, depending on their position within the bank's organization. Bank customers are only allowed to access the online banking client by using their customer number and a password as user credentials. Within their account they are also only entitled to the set of actions which need to be executed with compliance to the principle of least privilege. If a clerk or a customer issues a transaction (such as transferring money between accounts or opening a new account), their account must have the appropriate privilege both at the front end and the backend of the CBS. This is because the user needs to be logged as a responsible instance for the invocation of any service of the application server. Each transaction, conducted within the CBS either by a clerk, customer or administrator via one of the clients or through direct access, is generally logged in order to prevent unauthorized data manipulation. The log files are then transferred to a secured location which is only accessible by the revisors and are subject to regular reviews.

4.5.3.3 Information View

The data of the CBS is on the one hand stored in three different databases with the use of three different data schemes, and on the other hand in configuration files in the application server and the database server. It is classified depending on its nature.

- Business data: Business data is the core data, which is required to execute the use cases as needed from the customer bank. It comprises customer data, as well as account data, product data and all kinds of transaction data.
- Metadata: The metadata is a description of the business data and contains information which is not necessarily important for the users and their business processes, but is crucial for the operation of the CBS. A few examples of the metadata are the number of data records in a certain table, the number of accesses on a certain table or the size of a database. Metadata may not only be stored within the databases but can also be contained within infrastructure components.
- Logging Data: Usually transactions need to be recorded due to legal and internal revision requirements. In CBS, this is done through the use of so called Watchlists, which record every manipulation on any database field containing business data, regardless whether this was done through the business logic of the CBS (and hence either through a service- or a natural user) or an administrator who directly worked within the database. The logging data is then exported in order to be accessible for the internal revision department.
- Configuration Data: The configuration data is required for the operation of the CBS and is in parts stored within the databases, and in parts in infrastructural components. It contains information about how (with which parameters) the CBS is to be operated.

4.5.3.4 Data Flow

The data flow of the CBS is transaction based and centered around the user interfaces of the clients. If a user inserts data into a user interface and then triggers the processing (e.g. transferring money from one account to another via the online banking client), he initiates a use case containing one, or several data transactions. Within each transaction, the data is first validated in terms of its data format, length and logical format (e.g. the IBAN has to have a defined format). In case data in a required input field is missing or the data is inappropriate, the user will immediately receive an error message. If the data is complete and sound, it will be sent to the application server. Inside the application server it is once again validated from a functional perspective. E.g. it is verified whether the user is authorized to commit the transaction and whether they are compliant to any functional constraints, such as account limits or other business restrictions. If these verifications are positive, the data is processed according to the business logic of the triggered use case. In the course of the functional data checks and the functional processing, further data will be required which was not provided by the user. This data is fetched from the respective databases and then processed together with the input data. The result is then persisted in one, or several process steps (depending on the nature of the business case), and the outcome is then delivered to the client. The result may either be a simple message informing the user whether his operation was successful or not, or it may be a message which is also combined with further data such as a reduced account balance after he transferred cash from his account to another.

4.5.4 Implementation Architecture

In contrast to the logical architecture, the implementation structure concentrates on physical aspects of the CBS, such as the deployment and technologies.

4.5.4.1 Deployment

The deployment of the CBS occurs in several environments, depending on the requirements of the using bank. Usually there is at least one test or user acceptance test environment within each customer bank as well as a production environment, where the life data is situated. The test environment is regularly reset to a contemporary snapshot of the production system, including live data of the customers and their transactions. Each environment contains at least two Linux servers where the first one is the database server and the second one acts as application server. The scale of these servers depends on the load which they need to handle, however they also support clustering and load balancing. That means that the databases are deployed in several instances on several servers which are then grouped in a cluster. The cluster management performs the control of the database servers and regulates the replication of data between them. However, as in the case of the CBS, three different databases are used; the Core Banking, the CRM and the Private

Banking and each need to run in a separate cluster. In addition to the databases, the documents as well as the document import- and export location of the CBS are hosted on the same server.
The application server hosts the Core Banking application itself. The CRM tower is compiled and executed within a Java Virtual Machine, the private banking tower is compiled through a GNU compiler distribution and the Core Banking tower is compiled through an Infinite36 compiler. The components of the interface layer (Web Services and APIs) are deployed on a Tomcat web-server which is in turn hosted on the application server. The Tomcat webserver also contains the online banking client and enables a replication of the application server into several instances in connection with load balancing.

5 Proposed Technical Modernization Process for a CBS

Up to now, extensive knowledge regarding Core Banking Systems and their software architectures was gathered, and presented, and is the basis for the following proposed modernization process. This process begins with the scenario, where a technologically heterogeneous, and in parts outdated, CBS needs to be modernized.

In doing so, this process attempts to answer the second research question as defined in section 1.1 and defines a potential way of modernizing an existing Core Banking system, regardless of its existing architecture, functionality or technology stack. It is organized in sequential steps, which lead from the beginning into a recurring modernization cycle that should be considered as important element within the lifecycle of a CBS. The rationale behind the process character is to begin an ongoing modernization lifecycle, which makes sure that each functional component is architecturally renewed from time to time, in order to make sure that the overall CBS keeps up with the global technological evolution in terms of software technologies and architectures.

Overall, the following process as described in the following, utilizes the methodology proposed by the BIAN and extends it through an architectural modernization approach, which is not covered by the BIAN. Nevertheless, it retains the flexibility to exchange the BIAN through a different banking service landscape standard, in case this fits better to the requirements of a bank's business- and CBS architecture. The BIAN service landscape as described in section 4.2 serves as a benchmark providing a target architecture and is therefore contained in a sub step of this process, but this benchmark may also be provided through a different (customized) standard.

Except from that, this process is conceptualized under the premise that a CBS should functionally cover the uses cases, which are required by a bank and its organization. Due to the fact that each CBS and each using bank have their distinct specifics, this process remains independent of technologies and architectures, which implies that this process needs to be tailored to each CBS and also to the use cases and business architecture of every bank. Furthermore, it does not cover the details contained in a modernization module due to these specifics but is a generic framework to begin and maintain an ongoing modernization of information systems in the context of CBS. The requirement for ongoing modernization is given by the technological evolution as well as changing business requirements which surround CBS and constantly have an impact on it. Hence the proposed process is designed as cyclic approach since modernization should never stop and in order to reflect surrounding long term changes.

Therefore, from a methodological perspective each cycle encompasses the following steps:

- Assessment of the bank's current organization and service structure including planned strategic changes. This step is necessary, since the current- and future service structure of the bank must be incorporated into the modernization process.
- Assessment of the current CBS functionality in order to determine to what extent it matches the using bank's future needs and where additional functionality is needed.
- Based on the intended service structure and the current application baseline, a target architecture is created with the aim to define the intended functional amount and architecture of the modernized CBS.
- Next, the available modernization instruments need to be defined which are admissible to the CBS (depending on technological and resource influence factors). The selection of modernization instruments is necessary since it is a basic decision over the approach, how a CBS is to be architecturally modernized and depends on the technological specifics of the CBS and the resources of the bank or vendor.
- Sub sequentially they need to be assigned to the functional modules in order to determine, through what architectural instrument each functional module of the CBS shall be modernized.
- Then, the selected methodology needs to be compiled into a modernization strategy, outlining in what time schedule and sequence the CBS the modernization shall happen.
- In order to verify the admissibility of the modernization strategy and to ensure that the modernizations instruments work as planned a PoC phase must be conducted.
- If the PoC was successfully committed, further modules are to be modernized until the target architecture has been successfully realized. The target architecture is then the basis for the following modernization cycle.

Illustration 18 shows the high level approach of the following process.

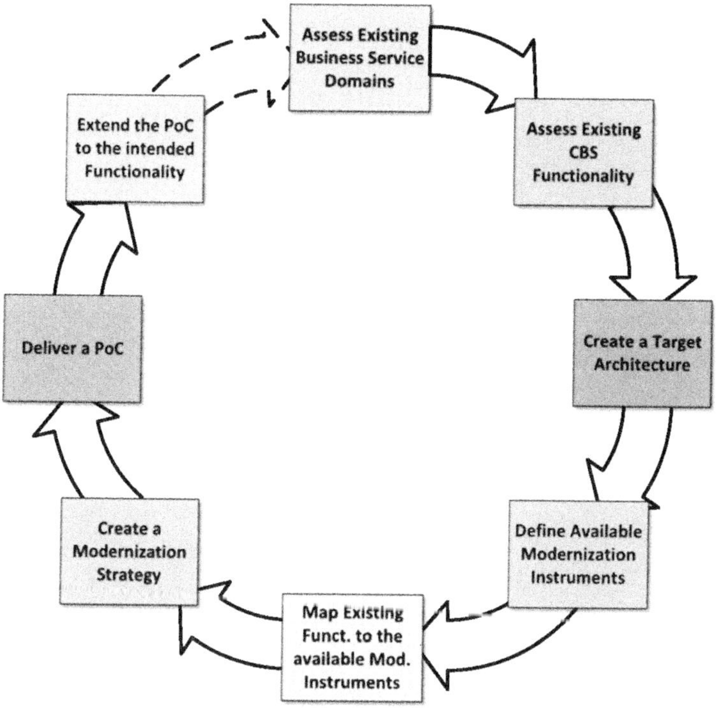

Illustration 18: Overview of the proposed Modernization Process

5.1 The Process Steps

As depicted in Illustration 18, the modernization process consists out of eight steps. They will be described in the following.

5.1.1 Assess existing business service domains

In general, a Core Banking System should reflect the business structure (service domains) of the using bank as it provides the bank with the information as well as the corresponding transformation functionality (business logic) to cover its main business processes. Assessing the existing business services of a bank in order to modernize the underlying CBS, is only applicable if the CBS' functionality is also maintained by a bank. In the situation that the CBS is fully developed and supported by a dedicated vendor, then the CBS as a framework is usually deployed within several bank institutes with different connected business use cases and requirements. Therefore, the vendor either needs to assess the existing business structure and requirements of its customers in order to derive a common business service landscape, or create a business service landscape for which it assumedly serves its customers best. In case the using bank develops and maintains its own CBS, the first process step contains the following sub steps:

1. Outline the organization of the Bank:
   Banks usually have already a well-defined internal structure that divides them into a number of subdivisions, branches and departments. These organizational units have a distinct field of tasks and are responsible for the execution of their specific field of work. If not already existent, the organizational units (OUs) and their business tasks need to be documented.

2. Create a process model of the Bank:
   In order to fulfil their specific tasks each organizational unit has a number of business processes, which are executed repeatedly. These processes are usually supported by various IT applications which form the majority of the bank's IT landscape. The core processes are mainly covered by sub functions of the CBS. The mapping between each OU's processes and use cases in connection with the CBS' functions need to be documented as well in order to elaborate which function of the CBS is used by which OU for which use case. The result is an enterprise blueprint which depicts the functional usage of the current CBS by the different OUs. Usually banks have already some kind of high level task description for their OUs. If this is the case, then the task description need to be elaborated to a detailed process models.

3. Future strategy:
   Each Bank usually possesses a long term strategy which is to be reflected both within its organization as well as in the supporting IT landscape. To realize that strategy, Banks recurringly perform internal organizational transformations. Respectively, the CBS modernization has to take these intended changes into account as they imply the future usage of the CBS. Therefore, the current enterprise blueprint needs to be modified accordingly. The overall result is a requirement document that contains a description of the business processes and the required functionality of the CBS according to the bank's long term future.

5.1.2 Assess existing CBS functionality

The next step comprises the assessment of the current CBS against the required functionality that as in the previous step. To do so, it is necessary to examine the current CBS architecture and to create a consistent functional topology of the entire framework as it currently is. CBS have already internal architecture description documents, however the focus of this step should lie in the division of the CBS into functional modules which may be examined on their own in the ensuing steps. In terms of practicality, the following steps are recommended:

1. Assess the current functions of the CBS:
   Each CBS has a certain amount of functionality which is required by the using bank. This functionality can be split up into functions that are on the one hand invoked by the user directly or on the other hand perform specific tasks for other functions. Accordingly, this step consists of the segmentation of the overall functionality into defined functions and yields a definition of the current functional coverage.

2. Raise the functional topology:
   Although CBS may be technologically severely outdated, they usually retain some sort of modularization in the form of separated programs, program bundles, components, services or even frameworks, which contribute to the CBS' functional stack. Determining which component is responsible for which functions results in a consistent mapping between code and the connected function and may uncover double implementations or unused components.

3. Raise interfaces:
   The previously raised functional components usually interact with each other through some kind of interfaces, such as the invocations of APIs, functions, web services or the combined transformation of data. Capturing the communication patterns between each component helps to reveal how tightly functions are coupled with each other, and is supportive information for the definition of a consistent set of functions for the desired CBS architecture.

4. Define a functional map for the legacy functionality (application baseline blueprint):
   Based on the previous steps, a functional blueprint of the existing CBS may be defined which contains a homogenized set of functions, the topology of these functions as well as their interactions. This blueprint documents the actual state of the CBS and is the baseline from which the transformation and modernization begins.

5. Assess functional coverage of the current architecture against business functions:
   In order to align the current CBS with the required (current and future) business processes, it needs to be benchmarked against them. That means, based on the application baseline, verification is required to define to what extent the CBS covers the current and

intended business processes, and hence the strategy of the using bank. In case there are functions missing, they may be considered for implementation during the modernization process. On the other hand, if there are functions which are no longer required, then they may be considered for decommissioning. The main result of this step should be a list of functional gaps and overhead of the CBS in comparison to the bank's functional requirements.

6. Version the application baseline:
   As the proposed modernization process is recurring, it is recommended to version the baseline, since it describes the functionality of the bank at a defined point of time including future modernization plans.

5.1.3 Create a target architecture according to the BIAN.

The aim of this process step is to create a target blueprint which is compliant to the BIAN standard [88]. It serves as should-be scenario, that applies to the CBS after its modernization. To do so, BIAN already provides a Guideline containing an outline how a BIAN compliant target architecture may be constructed. The overall approach as defined by the BIAN is illustrated in figure 19 and described in the sections 5.1.3.1 to 5.1.3.3.

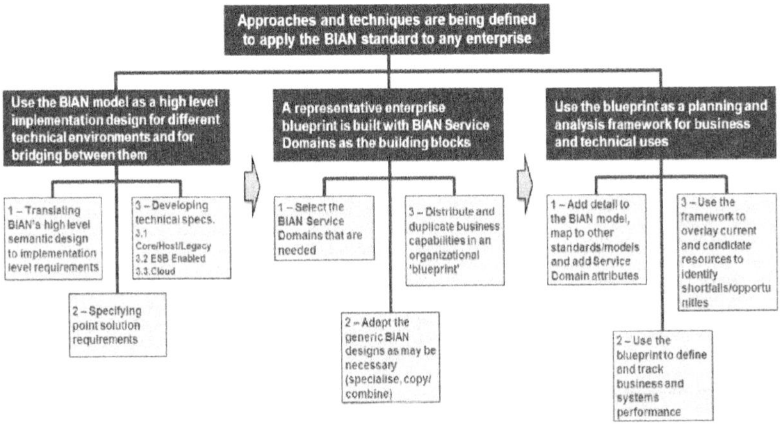

Illustration 19: Application of the BIAN standard [91]

5.1.3.1 Using the BIAN model as a high level implementation design

1. Translate BIAN's high level semantic designs to implementation level requirements:
   The BIAN has a number of high level design principles which need to be applied to a target architecture. The SOA paradigm is one of these principles, which is used with the aim to create the target architecture in a service oriented manner. Use of service domain clusters is also recommended in order to encapsulate related services into functional blocks. These service domain clusters shall be interpreted in the context of the actual technical environment which banks function in. These three environments are either a CBS which is a monolithic Host application, a CBS which is operated with the help of an Enterprise Service Bus (ESB) or a loosely coupled- or even cloud based CBS. Another semantic design principle is to map the business architecture to the technical architecture. In other words, a mapping the existing business architecture to service domains in order to directly link a service domain cluster with the consumer organization and its business processes needs to be done. BIAN only provides a high level implementation roadmap in order to apply its standard to an existing CBS architecture. Hence it recommends to extend its framework through detailed specifications, which reflect the bank's requirements as well as the actual architectural situation of the respective CBS. The final semantic design principle is the use of BIANs point solutions.

2. Specify Point Solution Requirements:
   Specifying Point Solution Requirements (= targeted requirements) according to the BIAN standard consists out of the following stages:
   a.) Develop Business Cases for the impact, which is derived out of the modernization or transformation of the CBS in terms of financial gain, performance, stability, etc.
   b.) Create Business Scenarios for the main business event which is going to be handled by the respective point solution requirement. The resulting list of business scenarios should cover all requirements for the CBS from the bank.
   c.) Connect the business scenarios to the required services of a service domain in order to specify a static representation of the service interaction. This can be done via wireframe models.

3. Develop Technical Specs:
   Depending on the environment in which a bank system performs (may be either a Host based, an ESB based or a cloud based core banking system) and according to the BIAN, technical specs need to be created which describe the intended functionality of a service

after its transformation on a functional- and technical level and under compliance of the previously defined implementation principles.

In the context of the proposed modernization process, the above three steps result in an already detailed technical specification of the functionality of the intended Core Banking System after its transformation.

5.1.3.2. Building a representative enterprise blueprint out of BIAN service blocks

1. Select the BIAN service domains (service blocks) that are needed:
   BIAN already contains a predefined set of service domains which depict the best practice allocation of functionality according to its standard. In that regard, the first step is to map the application baseline and the list of gaps and overheads, which were derived in the previous process step, to the BIAN's service domains, in order to specify which of them are necessary. This selection is a critical sub step within the modernization process as it may offer service domains which are not needed by the bank.

2. Adapt the generic BIAN designs as may be necessary (specialize, copy, combine, service domains):
   Next, the selected service domains need to be adapted, which means that they either need to be reduced to the functionality which is actually needed or extended in case the BIAN lacks aspects of functionality, determined in the application baseline. In some cases, service domains may be extended by required functional specialities of the bank's CBS or combined, to better serve the needs of the bank. The result of this step is a raw version of the target architecture that is compliant with the BIAN.

3. Distribute and duplicate business capabilities in an organizational blueprint:
   Finally, the service domains which were selected and adapted in the raw version need to be assembled and matched against the projected organization of the bank. BIAN proposes that this should be done by matching the service domains in the form of value chains to each business line (organization or business unit) in order to check whether all required functionality is considered and whether each service domain is needed by at least one business unit. In that regard, the BIAN service domains represent the functionalities (services) required to cover all use cases of the bank. During the process of matching, BIAN recommends to take both discrete lines of business operations (e.g. geographical lines, country organizations) where certain operations are done centrally in one business service

unit, as well as legal entity structures into account. Having completed the matching process, the result should be a raw mapping of functionality, in terms of service domains, to the intended business domains. As a consequence, the previously created specifications need to be adapted in order to fit to the mapping.

5.1.3.3. Using the enterprise blueprint as a basis for further analysis

BIAN suggests using the derived enterprise blueprint as an analysis framework where the blueprint shall help to identify critical-, or complex service domains and to measure performance. It proposes the following three steps:

1. Add detail to the BIAN model, map to other standards as well as models and add service domain attributes.
2. Use the blueprint to define and track business and systems performance.
3. Use the framework to overlay current-, and candidate resources to identify shortfalls and opportunities.

In terms of architecture, it is more vital to detail the derived service domains, in order to create a consistent target architecture based on the previously created specifications. Combined with the projected enterprise blueprint, they form the target architecture describing the functionality of the CBS after its transformation.

5.1.3.4. Version the Target Architecture

As soon as the target architecture has been created in the form of the projected enterprise blueprint in combination with the specifications of the included (customized) service domains, they need to be versioned, since they describe the future architecture of the CBS. Furthermore, after having reached the target architecture in through the modernization cycle, it will serve as the application baseline for the subsequent modernization cycle.

5.1.4 Define the available modernization instruments

Once the target architecture has been defined, it is necessary to outline the available techniques which are admissible for the modernization of a CBS. The number and nature of these techniques depends on the specifics of the target CBS, as some of them might be incompatible with a CBS due to technical, political or organizational reasons. The following list describes the main instruments which allow for the overall process to be open to custom modernization techniques. Naturally, this process also supports alternative versions of instruments described below. In general, there are two types of modernization instruments. First, the ones which pursue a big-bang approach with one major transformation step and second, the ones that perform an incremental modernization process with different modernization strategies (component based modernization, simultaneous modernization, roadmaps) [17].

5.1.4.1 Reverse Engineering and Model Driven Development

MDD is described in section 4.1.2 and may either be used in a process based, or in a big-bang based approach. It is suitable in situations where old, complex functions, for which no documentation exists, need to be modernized. Through its automated code analysis, it follows every logical path within a piece of code and abstracts it to a logical and technologically independent meta-Model. The meta-model then serves as logical and complete documentation of the existing code and may then be transformed in order to be re-implemented under the use of a different software architecture [45, 46]. This approach is on the one hand flexible as only components of the legacy functionality may be modernized and on the other hand, if needed, the entire system may be re-implemented before being sent into operation (big-bang approach). Furthermore, it is also compatible to parallel and roadmap based modernization strategies. The overall scheme for MDD modernization looks as follows [78]:

1. First a portion of functionality that is subject to modernization is selected. Its source code is then analysed and abstracted into a technology and platform independent meta-model.
2. Next, the meta-model is transformed into a target model, which satisfies the requirements of the desired architecture.
3. The target model is then implemented in a certain programming language (may be a different language as well as the language of the legacy component).
4. As soon as the implementation is done, it is necessary to verify the behaviour of the newly implemented software component against the legacy component. This can be done through extensive testing.

5.1.4.2 Architectural Replacement:

Architectural Replacement may also be conducted using different strategies, however as a modernization instrument, there are a number of different facilities offered with the purpose of replacing existing legacy functionality or architecture [92, 34]:

1. Reimplementation: The first option is to manually re-implement the legacy code under the use of an architecture which fits the required benchmarks. The implicated effort apparently strongly correlates to the size and complexity of the legacy functionality and is only possible when enough documentation exists.

2. Buying and Customizing: If a different product that is in line with the architectural requirements is available on the market, then it is a valid option to buy it, customize it and to integrate it into the existing CBS. This requires implementation work as well, however, the amount depends on the functional Delta between the existing functionality and the required functionality of the new component. Nevertheless, this approach might be cheaper than completely re-implementing the legacy component. A drawback of this approach is, that the obtained component may extend the technology stack of the CBS and its source code may not be available to the integrating party. Hence, it may become a black-box within the CBS service landscape which cannot be directly controlled by the CBS developers.

In terms of architectural replacement, the overall admission pattern looks as follows [39]:

1. In the first step, a component is picked which shall be modernized.
2. Next, evaluation is needed on whether reimplementation or the customization and integration of a related existing product is preferable.
3. Once this is done, the new component needs to be integrated into the existing system and its behaviour needs to be tested against the behaviour of the legacy component in order to verify their functional equivalence.
4. After the equivalence is ensured, the legacy component can be decommissioned and be removed from the CBS.

5.1.4.3 Architecture Refactoring & Transformation:

Refactoring is usually done within an iterative process where the components of a CBS are refactored one after another or in parallel, depending on the modernization strategy. Architectural refactoring happens on both architectural- and code level, whereas architectural refactoring is a top down approach and code refactoring is a bottom up approach. In this context Architectural refactoring always involves code refactoring as the source code implements the overlying architecture [34]. The main aim of architectural refactoring is to remove old architectural traces and to execute architectural changes (as is the case with architectural modernization). Refactoring can generally be carried out as a part of an architectural roadmap approach or any other iterative strategy. The workflow pattern is as follows:

1. First, choose a component which is to be modernized iteratively, however it should be taken into account that the selected component may also have a number of subcomponents.

2. Next, its architecture needs to be understood (covered in section 5.1.2), and a target architecture needs to be created (refer to the previous section). These two architectures create a Delta, which needs to be overcome in one or more incremental refactoring cycles. These refactoring cycles should be planned within a refactoring plan or strategy, and they must be monitored in order to ensure a refactoring in the desired direction.
3. Each refactoring step results in a temporary sub architecture, which should be versioned and tracked appropriately. Except from that, it should also be versioned.
4. Depending on the test strategy and its size, the refactored component should either be tested after each refactoring step against the architectural requirements or after the completion of the overall refactoring process.

5.1.4.4 Decommissioning of old Functionality

The easiest way to modernize architectures in the context of CBS, is to decommission functionalities which are still a part of the CBS but are no longer in use, due to changing user requirements as well as environmental circumstances. The advantage of decommissioning in connection to CBS modernization is that the overall architecture is cleaned of unused components. Furthermore, its size and complexity are reduced and the maintainability of the architecture and the remaining source code is increased. Hence, simply reducing a CBS by its unused components is a valid modernization instrument. Components that are not subject to the bank's business cases are determined during the assessment of existing CBS functionality against the bank's organization (see section 5.1.2).

5.1.5 Map existing functionality to the modernization instrument

The next step of the modernization process is to decide through which modernization instrument each portion of the application baseline should be modernized. The result of this step should be a mapping of defined functional segments to a modernization instrument or alternatively, if required, a combination of modernization instruments. The decision of which instrument shall be used depends on a number of technical-, and in parts also business, criteria which need to be defined as well. The criteria may then be used to rank several appropriate alternatives against each other and to create a justification why a certain modernization instrument has been used in order to transform a functional portion. A practical method would be to gather an expert round of architects or key technicians, who know the functionality outlined by the application baseline (the "old" code) and the specific pitfalls and potential workarounds. They can then be consulted in order to assign a requirement and technology related score to each of the criteria and to give each modernization instrument a ranking of how applicable it is to a functional portion which is to be modernized. The following criteria count to the common aspects that play a role in terms of modernization [34]:

- **Complexity and structure:**
  The main criteria is the complexity of the old functionality that ultimately decides about the workforce and the time required to modernize a portion. If the structure of the code is already decoupled and works according to the same architectural principle, then a (semi) automated transformation via a model driven development tool might be applicable. However, if the code is grown over years and has a large number of internal dependencies, then architectural replacement through re-implementation or purchasing a new customized product to replace the old one is more suitable.

- **Available Knowledge and Documentation:**
  In larger Information Systems, such as Core Banking Systems, there are often functional portions which are decades old with the original engineer who created them no longer available as well as no documentation being left behind. If no other engineers understand the internal architecture and mechanisms of the old code, then an automated transformation is bears risks. That means, if there is a lot of knowledge available about the old code, then an automated and manual transformation combined with the decommissioning unused parts are legitimate ways to modernize old code. However, if the knowledge is inaccessible and there is no documentation about the old code (it is run using the "never touch a running system" principle), then architectural replacement is to be considered.

- **Functional size:**
  The next key criteria is the size of the old portion, measured in lines of code. The larger the outdated portion is, the more manpower and time is required to manually refactor it and to develop it to a successor software architecture. Therefore (semi) automated transformation procedures are a way to lower costs and effort after a comparably large initial effort for modelling (model driven software transformation requires the creation of a meta model). If the portion is too large, it is a valid alternative to evaluate the market for newer existing products which might be customized in order to fulfil the functions of the outdated portion. On the other hand, if the portion is smaller, a manual refactoring, or even manual rewriting is a more resource saving approach.

- **Analysability:**
  Analysability as a criteria is related to complexity with the difference that there might be code portions which are not directly available for inspection (e.g. since only the executa-

bles are available and not the source code). In that case, reverse engineering and subsequent model based reimplementation is a way to cope with applications which are hard to analyse. Via reverse engineering, logical paths may be processed through a meta model, which is then the basis for reimplementation in any desired technology. On the other hand, if there is enough documentation and knowledge about the code available, any other modernization instrument may be used depending on the other criteria chosen for assessment.

- **Estimated Cost:**

  As criteria the estimated cost of modernization is a decision item specific to the outdated portion and depends highly on the other given criteria. Furthermore, the estimated cost is normally a rough estimation, as the real costs often change massively in the course of a transformation.

  In general, manual refactoring, reimplementation or replacement are often the cheapest way to modernize a piece of code, depending on who does the manual implementation work. Automated- or semi-automated tools on the other hand usually require major costs in their initial phase, during the creation of a meta model of the existing code and an emulator that is capable of automatically transforming old code into a new desired technology. However, in the longer term, transformation supported by automated means brings decisive savings in terms of cost, manpower and time. The third option of buying and customizing a similar but newer product is usually an expensive way to modernize old functionality that also depends on the exact functionality which is to be replaced.

- **Time effort:**

  In terms of time effort manual reimplementation of the outdated code is a more time intensive modernization instrument, depending on the size of the portion which is to be modernized. Hence, automated modernization tools may bring a decisive advantage in the longer term, especially when the functionality is of a large scale.

- **Supported Technologies and Transformability:**

  Some outdated portions of code are sometimes not transformable due to technical constraints. For instance, when an old technology, which has never been updated or superseded by a newer variant, is used. In this circumstance, architectural refactoring or transformation as well as automated means are not applicable and architectural replacement methods need to be considered.

5.1.6 Create a modernization strategy

After the application baseline, a target architecture and a mapping are created that clarify, how the modernization shall transpire. To do so a modernization strategy is needed as it elaborates the time schedule and in what order the overall modernization along with its sub-modernizations shall take place. It is recommended to take the application baseline as well as the modernization mapping and examine their dependencies. The sequence of dependencies as well as additional factors (such as priority or complexity) then define a sequence depicting which module needs to be modernized in its own modernization stream as well as when. That sequence may then be used in order to create a time plan which looks similar to a GANTT chart which is utilised as a master strategy in the modernization blueprint which orchestrates the entire modernization effort. Next, each modernization stream contained in the blueprint modernization principles is defined, including the preconditions and post conditions necessary for the modernization procedure to begin and be considered complete respectively. These post conditions may be of various kinds, such as technical-, qualitative-, functional- and non-functional constraints. Common valid post conditions would be the following:

- The module needs to comply with the target architecture.
- The required functional use cases of the legacy module need to be implemented and possess the same behaviour (+ potential change requirements) as its legacy module.
- The behaviour of the modernized module needs to be successfully tested against its target architecture as well as the same test cases as the legacy module.

Aside from its pre- and post-conditions each module also needs to have a mapping to the legacy module, that was the basis on which it was transformed or which it shall replace. The resulting modernization blueprint is then a central document which enables tracking as well as a consistent orchestration of the entire modernization cycle.

Once the strategy has been established, the modernization needs to be versioned as it is the central roadmap in order to achieve the target architecture from the baseline of applications onwards.

5.1.7. Deliver a PoC and test it

In general it is possible to run several modernization cycles in parallel on one CBS (see section 5.2 in terms of the process granularity), however it is recommended to perform a Proof of Concept (PoC) that ascertains, that the overall modernization concept is valid and works in practice. The PoC is not necessarily required in order to conduct the overall modernization, but is nevertheless an opportunity to learn from the modernization strategy and to refine it accordingly before the entire modernization is applied on the CBS. To commence the PoC, it is recommended to select an exemplary outdated module from the application baseline. It should be separable from the other modules and (in the best case) either work on its own after its modernization or be capable of interacting with the legacy system in order to fulfil its business purpose. Additionally, the selected module should be functionally representative and should not be a trivial module to modernize in order to maximize the learning curve for the entire modernization cycle. And it should not use a means of architectural refactoring as modernization instrument in order to be revertible, in case that needs to be done. Instead it should either use an automated or architectural replacement approach as both ways create a separate result which sub sequentially will substitute its outdated predecessor.

Next, the selected PoC module needs to be modernized to the target architecture as given in the modernization strategy. If any complications turn up during its modernization which have their root cause in the strategy, then it should be adapted accordingly. Also technical-, organizational- or business constraints which were previously unconsidered but come to display unforeseen effects during the PoC modernization should be taken account of, and included in the modernization strategy.

After the modernization had been done, it must be tested in order to verify that it has the same behaviour as its predecessor. Regression tests are an effective way as they directly compare the behaviour of the modernized software with the behaviour of the old one. In case of functional deltas occurring, the modernization either needs to be completed or even changed. For instance, model based modernization is prone to errors in the beginning as the underlying meta model may be inconsistent or contain logical errors. Therefore, an emulator that technically emulates old code into new code according to a meta model usually requires several refinement cycles before being able to transform code with an accuracy of nearly 100% [78].

Aside from regression tests, the PoC module should also be verified internally through further unit tests or component tests and its architecture needs to be examined, in order to make sure that it actually complies to the target specification as specified in the architecture (see section 5.1.3). Finally, the PoC module needs to be integrated into the CBS in order to effectively replace its outdated predecessor. From a testing perspective, this can be verified through integration tests and end to end system tests including the PoC module. Finally, the PoC module needs to be integrated into the release plan of the CBS to effectively come into service. Usually each CBS is developed within at least two or three environments (a development environment, a testing or UAT environment and a production environment with usage of live data) whereas functional deployments are made into the production environment within coordinated releases or updates.

5.1.8. Extend the PoC and retest it

As soon as the PoC had been completed, the learnings of it need to be included into the modernization strategy. The PoC is also a decision basis which shows, whether the modernization of the entire CBS scope is achievable or whether major adaptions need to be done.

If the entire modernization strategy is deemed to be a feasible real life approach then the PoC may be extended step by step according to the strategy document, its time plan as well as the mapping between functional portions and modernization instruments. Throughout and after their modernization the modules need to be tested in the same manner as the PoC module through regression tests, internal white box unit tests and integration tests, both with the legacy system and through integration tests with the preceding new modules which were modernized prior to them. And in the same manner as the PoC, they also need to be checked against their respective specification from the target architecture in order to verify whether they are compliant to it. In terms of modernization, the integration of modules which were updated through architectural refactoring is different from modules that are replaced by superseding modules, as they are not a replacement but rather an updated version of their outdated preceding module. Like the PoC, modules finally need to be integrated into the CBS' release plan in order to come into effect.
Depending on the time, scale and functional scope of the modernization, the extension of the PoC will usually stretch over several releases of a CBS, as it is an ongoing process. However, the advantage of this approach is, that on the one hand several modernization cycles may be executed on one CBS with disjunctive scopes and on the other hand within each cycle each modernization module may be modernized in parallel or in a defined series, relative to the other modules depending on whether it has technological-, or functional reliance on any other module.
As soon as all intended functional portions, which were planned for modernization, reach the modernized state and are successfully tested against the specifications of the target application, the entire modernization process is considered to be complete.

5.1.9. Keep up the modernization work.

In general, it is recommendable to constantly conduct modernization work on a Core Banking System in order to keep it technologically and architecturally up to date. However, the time period in which a particular function or code portion should be updated strongly depends on the technology on which it is implemented as well as the modernity of its architecture. Hence, years or decades may pass until the next time a piece of functional behaviour is modernized. Nevertheless, the proposed modernization framework supports recurring modernization cycles through versioning the baseline of applications and the target architecture, which sooner or later becomes the baseline of applications in a future modernization cycle. In theory, a modernization cycle could potentially start over and over again and therefore reflects the principle of continuous improvement and modernization. Yet in practice, due to business constraints (modernization work requires financial resources, manpower and time which would, from a business perspective, rather be invested in developing more functional value), modernization is viewed mainly as a necessary malady. But all in all and especially in the branch of Core Banking Systems, old technologies consistently impose more technical constraints on newly generated functions which are subject to more sophisticated technological requirements. Therefore, the pressure of getting away from old legacy code becomes more pressing as more time passes. In order to avoid future restrictions due to old architectures and technologies, a continuous modernization process that constantly occupies a certain percentage of resources is more sustainable in the long life of a (already complex) Core Banking System than so called "big bang operations" that in turn bear more risk. It can be said with certainty that no modernization at all, will deem a Core Banking System unusable in the long term, since an outdated CBS requires more maintenance and gets more and more incapable to support the ongoing technological evolution, since the technological distance increases over time.

5.2. Process Properties

After the process steps were outlined in the previous section, the main properties it possesses will be discussed at this point.

Top Down Approach:
Generally, the proposed modernization process is a top down approach, as it first examines a bank's organization and strategy and then derives a target architecture on that basis. Furthermore, it first takes the overall organizational picture of a bank and then drills down to individual functions and components in the Core Banking system. In that context it is also aligned to the BIAN, which follows a similar approach.

Flexibility:
One of the main features of this process is its flexibility as well as adaptability in terms of its sub-procedures. The core definition of the process consists out of the sequence of its eight sub-steps and their application, with the steps themselves also open to adaption. That means, that it can be arbitrarily amended depending on the needs of an implementing bank or CBS vendor. In fact, if necessary, BIAN does not need to be used as the definition of a target architecture as there is no obligation for a bank to comply with BIAN. Instead, a different target architecture and a different method to derive a target architecture may be utilised. In terms of the chosen modernization instruments, the process is open to customization since if one of them is not suitable for a CBS' circumstances, it may be omitted or it may be swapped with a different modernization technique. Also, the delivery of a PoC is not an obligation before commencing a full-fledged CBS transformation. The proof of concept of the proposed process is essentially a low level verification method showing whether a planned modernization approach is admissible in reality or not. In that regard, the scope and the method of the PoC as well as the functionality which is probed in that PoC is

subject to custom choice. Furthermore, the extension of the PoC needs to be refined and scheduled based on a common project management process model such as the waterfall model, v-model or an agile project management method.
In the context of time, the process is flexible as each function or component is individually transformed in parallel to other functions, based on its own specifications and the most fitting modernization approach. That means, that the overall process framework orchestrates the modernization but leaves enough freedom for any special constraints which are liable to a certain function.

Extendibility and Adaptability:
As the proposed process is already an extension of the BIAN on a technical level, this process may be extended through further steps if this is more suitable for the needs of a CBS and its developers. Furthermore, the process steps as described in section 5.1, may be extended themselves as well, if this is required.

Granularity and Adaptability of functional Scope:
Another attribute of the proposed modernization process is its granularity. Its scope is adaptable and the size of the portions which are to be modernized may be altered depending on the specific environment where the modernization takes place. In theory, the granularity can be drawn down to the level of single routines which are modernized one by one, using their own modernization instrument. However, the proposed framework can also cover an entire Core Banking System which is modernized in one procedure. Hence, it is comparably easy to select different portions of different sizes which are considered as functional components to be transformed with the only constraint being, that they need to fit into the topology of the target architecture. This granularity also leaves the freedom to only modernize certain portions of the CBS at a time according to their own time plan and pace as well as their own modernization instruments.
In addition, it is also possible to allocate different sub functions of the original CBS to different modernization cycles as outlined at the beginning of this chapter. This implies the freedom to transform portions in independent modernization streams into different target architectures under the preconditions that there are no technical dependencies between the modernization streams and that it is compatible with the strategy of the using bank.

Recurrency:
The process may be recurrent, but it does not have to be. That means, a CBS or its sub functions may be transformed to a target architecture where any further modernization activity could be halted as soon as the entire target architecture is covered. Nevertheless, as modernization in theory should be a repeating process, the proposed process supports continuous modernization. In this case, the target architecture turns into a description and documentation of the application baseline and is hence the basis for another transformation cycle. If the transformation scope changes to

different functionalities (or a subset of the functionality modernized in the first cycle), this should be supported as well as the new target set of functions should already have been modularized in the first transformation cycle (if BIAN was used as target architecture). Therefore, the second modernization round should be easier to conduct, especially on a technical level.

Ongoing modernization Process:

The proposed modernization process is integrateable as a separate stream into other development cycles. That means, while for instance 80% of the developers supporting a CBS work on the usual support or on creating more value, the modernization process can also run as a side stream, which is either equipped with its own project management or integrated into the overall development activities and their governing project management. In that regard, it may be perceived as an ever-lasting activity as modernization in terms of long living and growing Information Systems should never stop.

Traceability:

Due to the versioning of a target architecture, the underlying software may be traced in its lifetime. Specifically, if a certain portion of business logic was transformed for instance from one language to another one in a different architecture, the origin of the functionality may be traced back, due to the versioning of the application baseline as well as the connected target architectures.

Agility and Process Focus:

The proposed modernization procedure is process driven, since each modernization of a separated portion of functionality is, in principle, a sub process of the overall modernization effort. Both agility as well as agile project management are supported throughout this cycle due to the separation of the modernization streams and its cyclic attribute. The use of scrum methodologies or other agile methods could be specifically imposed on each modernization stream.

May adopt different Architectural Modernization strategies:

In terms of modernization strategies, the process is open to alternatives or new modernization strategies, as long as the outdated module is covered by the baseline of applications and considered in the target architecture. In its current version, service oriented architectures, such as the BIAN, are used as an intended target architecture. However, it could be replaced by any other target architecture if that is more desirable for a using CBS.

Gathers several modernization efforts:

Except from its integrability and adaptability, another advantage is, that due to its flexibility and open character, the proposed approach is capable of governing multiple modernization streams of separate software functions that do not necessarily interact with each other but run in parallel or sequentially. Through the central governance, one modernization strategy's common measures or guidelines could be imposed on each modernization stream. Examples of these measures include; common performance indices showing empirically how "good" a modernization effort works and qualitative guidelines which could become effective during testing. Therefore, the process could be used as a basis for controlling purposes, but also as a basis for other technical- or business frameworks in order to better integrate it into its using organization.

Follows a divide and conquer approach:
The process framework already uses a divide and conquer approach in terms of modernization. Correspondingly, the legacy CBS is divided into modules which are then modernized in separated modernization streams. The implication of that is, that each stream may be treated on its own under the use of a different modernization instrument, depending on the technical nature of each module. Nevertheless, the divide and conquer approach opens the opportunity to examine each module on its own, and also allows the process to focus on a certain modernization stream (if necessary) in case problems turn up with it. Furthermore, this approach is already a topological preparation towards a modularized, and hence easier to maintain, target architecture.

5.3. Advantages and Disadvantages

Now that the process itself has been described and evaluated in terms of its properties, its advantages will be discussed in the following section. They are also put in context with other modernization approaches which are available in expert literature.

Consistent Roadmap:
One major advantage of the proposed process is, that due to its flexibility, it also takes the business environment into account. Its adaptability enables this procedure to be used in different Core Banking setups and depicts how an existing CBS may be developed to a more up to date architecture. Additionally, it is not only integrated with architectural target benchmarks, but also reflects future strategies of a using bank (or vendor), due to the approach that a target architecture should encompass and functionally support the future organization and strategy of a using organization. Other software and architecture modernization approaches are often concentrated on the technology of their approach only. However on the other hand, the proposed modernization is more high level and not thoroughly detailed technically. Instead, it takes the current and future environment into account and views architectural modernization not just as a single effort but rather as ongoing process which is a critical factor to the technological long term survival of a CBS.

Highly integrate able in existing software Engineering Setups:

Another advantage of the proposed modernization process is its integrate ability in existing CBS setups, as it not only supports one technical modernization approach but several, which are all also adaptable according to a CBS' specific needs. In addition to its functional adaptability, it may be extended or minimised as required, which deems it also adaptable in terms of its scope.

Technology and Architecture Independent:

The proposed process in its current state is technology independent and hence technologically applicable for every Core Banking System, regardless of its used technologies. Furthermore, it is also independent of any existing architecture but nevertheless capable of modernizing them with consideration of their complexity and adaptability.

Consistent Process Framework, which needs to be extended by some Project Management:

The modernization process currently lacks a consistent project setup as well as any kind of project management. In reality, a modernization effort is usually embedded into a separate project which manages the actions that need to be done and the environment in which a project is executed. Furthermore, a modernization requires resources, resource planning, financial funds and backup from the governing business. In its current form, this process does not guarantee, that as it is a plainly technical approach. Hence, it needs to be supplemented with a business framework containing a project management to ensure the proper execution of this technical modernization approach.

Incorporates a PoC:

A further strength of this process is that it incorporates and supports a PoC. This is necessary in order to test the theoretical planning (modernization blueprint, and target architecture) in practice and to return first learnings from practice into the modernization strategy in order to refine it before the majority of modernization tasks are committed.

Leaves a Number of Decisions Open:

The process framework is basically a proposal, which in its current state, is not detailed but still very flexible due to its design. Therefore, it leaves a large number of decisions open which highly depend on the organization and the requirements of the CBS vendor and using organization. As a consequence, it leaves a lot of space for wrong decisions, which may in turn occur due to inexperience in terms of software modernization, technical- and financial misjudgements, as well as missing considerations. Hence, it is highly recommended to gather experience from existing modernization projects and to put this modernization process next to other approaches in order to evaluate it, before applying it to the system.

Drawback of Flexibility:

The fact that the proposed modernization process is flexible, open, extendable and adaptable is in general a good characteristic. However, it also contains unintentional hazards, for instance, the flexibility opens doors to misuses, wrong assumptions as well as usage purposes for which the process was not intended. In turn that (technical) misuse could result in major economic and functional damage to a system which was modernized or transformed in a malicious way. Hence, it is important to verify this process among other process frameworks, and to verify its results as early as possible.

Missing Modularization:

From an architectural point of view, CBS are complex and large scale systems and their internal functionalities are often deeply interwoven among each other, incorporating a large number of functional and technical dependencies. Old CBS are often monolithic frameworks with few or virtually no modularization in them. Therefore, in each modernization project the modularization of such a monolith as a precondition for modernization is already a major project on its own. This modernization process does not address this issue as it assumes that a system has already been modularized. A solution to this problem would be to include a separate modularization step right after the assessment of the existing functionality (see section 5.1.2), which only deals with methodologies to split architectural monoliths into functional parts. However, covering that would extends the scope of this thesis. Nevertheless, dealing with functional separation is a precondition upon which the proposed modernization process relies heavily.

6. Evaluation of the Modernization Process

After depicting the modernization process and having discussed its strongpoints and weak points in theory, this chapter deals with the practical evaluation of the proposed process. To do so, the exemplary outdated architecture as described in section 4.5will be applied to the process. As soon as the process reaches the stage of module wise modernization, the application will be continued on a selected submodule of the legacy CBS (in this case Day-End Processing) as describing the modernization of all legacy functionality would exceed the scope of this thesis. Next, the process as well as its application will be shown to experts in the field of core banking in order to find out whether this process has practical shortfalls. The scientific aspect of the evaluation was commenced via guided qualitative expert interviews. The interview guideline is attached in Appendix A and the interview transcripts are added in Appendix B.

6.1. Applying the Modernization Process on the exemplary Architecture

The application of the exemplary architecture, is structured according to the process steps as defined in section 5.1. Therefore, each of the following subsections covers one process step.

6.1.1. Assessment of existing Business Service Domains

The first step of the modernization process is to raise the organizational structure of a Bank which uses a particular CBS and gather the Core Banking business processes, that are executed within each organization unit. Additionally, the long term strategy and structure of the Bank needs to be taken into account with the purpose of aligning the future CBS with the future strategy of the Bank. How the current-, and prospected future organization is constructed depends on the using bank. However, in order to fulfil this step, a hypothetical future organization, which serves the purpose of the practical evaluation, will be assumed. It shall look as follows:

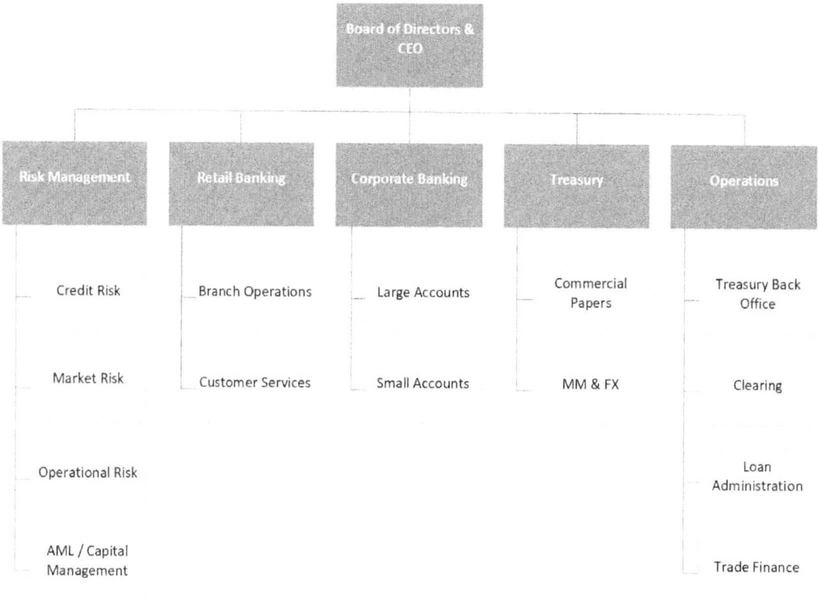

Illustration 20: Exemplary Organization of a Bank

According to its organization, the Bank has a focus on retail banking as well as corporate banking. The retail banking division contains the branch management, as well as the direct customer support, consisting out of private customer advice at the cash desk, and online support via the bank's internet channels. Corporate banking focuses on business customers which are divided into large customers and small customer companies. Aside from the retail and corporate banking business, it contains a treasury portion covering stock trading and money management. Furthermore, it incorporates a back office (operations) which is responsible for account current and maintenance tasks as well as a risk department. In practice, a bank usually has additional departments that do not directly use a CBS, such as a Human Resources department, a Finance and Payroll and an IT organization. Also, an internal revision and a compliance department are included as part of a bank organization.

6.1.2. Assessment of existing CBS functionality

After having the bank's organization raised, the CBS' functional topology needs to be elaborated. In the case of the exemplary architecture, as described in chapter 4.5. This was already done to a certain degree since it is already structured into a four layer architecture, which is further split up into functional modules. Under the assumption that the functional modules, as depicted in Illustration 20Illustration 17 are decoupled on code level, and interact with each other via interfaces, they may be adopted as a feasible overall structure. In this context, each module within the application tier contains a set of functions which are required to cover the necessary business processes of the bank. The sum of all functions defines the functional entirety of the CBS where each function may be either manifested within a program, a class, a single method or a set of methods (in case the code is object oriented). For instance, the account current module consists (among others) out of the following functions:

- End-of-Day, End-of-Month and Year-End Processing
- Calculation of daily Balances
- Calculation of Interest Rates (in various forms)
- Account keeping (depending on the kind of account – Giro-, Saving or Inventory)
- And many further functions.

After the functional topology had been summarized in the form of a distinct set of functions, their interfaces and dependencies need to be raised. In the current case, the loan module will be tightly connected to the customer scoring module as the customer scoring has a strong influence on the loan conditions of each customer. Accordingly, the loan module will either access the customer scoring module via API calls, web services or direct function invocations, or may simply access data in the CRM database which had been previously processed by the customer scoring module. Those interfaces need to be documented for each function of the CBS.

The sum of the derived functions as well as their dependencies and interfaces then need to be gathered within a functional map which is the application baseline blueprint (for illustration purposes, the exemplary application baseline blueprint for the Day-End Processing function of the given architecture is added in Appendix C). This blueprint will subsequently be benchmarked against the intended organization of the bank in order to identify functionality which is missing as well as functions which are no longer of use and may be considered for decommission. In the case of the given CBS architecture the benchmark delivers the following (high level) result on a module level:

Module	**State**	**Required by**
Core Banking		
Electronic Funds Transfer	existent	Branch Operations, Customer Services, MM&FX, Clearing, Loan Administration, Trade Finance
Account Current	existent	Branch Operations, Large Account, Small Accounts, Clearing, Treasury Back Office
Private- / Corporate Loans	existent	Large Accounts, Small Accounts, Credit Risk, AML / Capital Management, Loan Administration, Clearing
Card Management	existent	Branch Operations, Customer Services, Loan Administration

CRM		
Customer Management	existent	Branch Operations, Customer Services, Large Accounts, Small Accounts
Customer Core Data	existent	Branch Operations, Customer Services, Large Accounts, Small Accounts
Customer Scoring / Account Management	existent	Branch Operations, Customer Services, Large Accounts, Small Accounts, Credit Risk, Market Risk, Operational Risk
Document Management	existent	All Suborganisations
Customer Services	not existent	Customer Services, Branch Operations
Private Banking		
Order-/Portfolio Management	existent	Commercial Papers, Treasury Back Office, Trade Finance
Asset Management	existent	Commercial Papers, Treasury Back Office, Trade Finance
Market Data Modeling	existent	Market Risk
Customer Risk Management	existent	Branch Operations, Customer Services, Large Accounts, Small Accounts, Credit Risk, Market Risk, Operational Risk
Asset Liability Management	existent	Clearing, Loan Administration, AML / Capital Management
Risk Management	not existent	Credit Risk, Market Risk, Operational Risk
Trade and Investment	not existent	Trade Finance, MM&FX, Commercial Papers

Table 1: High Level Benchmark Result of existing vs. required Functionality

In this case, most modules required by the banks organization are existent within the CBS. Further analysis is necessary for each module in order to determine which sub-functions in each module are in fact needed and which are not needed. In addition, at least three modules which should cover the core business processes of the risk departments, as well as the departments centred on trade and investment are missing. A customer services component enabling the bank to integrate more customer interactions with the underlying CBS is also required. But all in all, the given table is a benchmark containing a mapping between the bank's organizational units and the CBS modules depicting where functionality is required and where given functionality (likely in an outdated technology and architecture) is available.

Finally, the derived application baseline blueprint, as well as the benchmark against the raised bank organization need to be versioned. This is done as they document the existing functionality and topology of a CBS and the functional gaps which are to be satisfied, in order to fulfil the requirements of the using bank.

6.1.3. Creation of a Target Architecture

In the previous section, the existing functionality as well as the gaps in the intended target have been identified. Based on these results, a target architecture that is compliant to the BIAN standard needs to be defined. To keep the scope of this thesis in a reasonable extent, this is only done conceptually via the outlined End-of-Day processing as given in Appendix C. To do so, the first step is to apply the BIANs service oriented high level design to the End-of-Day processing. Therefore, the End-of-Day processing needs to be classified into the BIAN's service landscape (currently in version 7.0) [53]. In the service landscape, the End-of-Day processing fits into the Service Domain "Financial Statements" under the "Finance" service domain cluster of "Business Support". According to BIAN, this Service Domain is "responsible for the consolidation and reporting of the audited financial statements of the enterprise (and its subsidiaries) including the balance sheet, statement of cash flows, statement of retained earnings and the income statement" [50]. In that Service Domain, the End-of-Day Processing are summarized together with the other (End-of-Month or Year-End) settlement processes as well as all functionality belonging to financial settlements and statements of the bank. The point solution requirements then need to be captured in the form of Business Cases, Business scenarios, and a mapping of business scenarios to the required business services as given within the End-of-Day-processing. In terms of the modernization of an existing End-of-Day routine, the main requirement is, that the transformed process has exactly the same functionality as the legacy process, however with some behavioural differences which need to be specified by the bank. This needs to be captured accordingly in the point solution requirements. The business case for the End-of-Day-process is the daily settlement of the sub ledger (in the form of the customer's giro and savings accounts), including the processing of all standing orders and transactions, as well as the subsequent settlement of the general ledger. A potential tactic to split up the Day-End-process into a service oriented topology is to recreate its functions as given in Appendix C in a service oriented architecture. On that basis, further technical specifications need to be created, to describe each intended service within the Day-End processing on its own as well as its interactions to other services. In any case, the technical specifications highly depend on the individual characteristics of the legacy implementation of the Day-End processing and possible additional requirements of the bank. In general, they should contain the following items:

- A use case description
- A specification of all interfaces and dependencies per subroutine
- Functional and Non-Functional Requirements
- A conceptual architecture
- A logical Architecture including the logical Data Flows and required data items
- An implementation Architecture including a technology stack and architectural directives in terms of logging, error handling, interface communication and security.

Next, the entire application baseline blueprint needs to be mapped to the service domain structure as specified by the BIAN. In the case of the given CBS, the existing modules can be mapped to the following service domains (the detailed mapping is contained in Appendix D).

Legacy CBS Module	**BIAN Service Domain Cluster**
Core Banking - Electronic Funds Transfer	Payments
Core Banking - Account Current	Product Management
	Account Management
	Regulations & Compliance
Core Banking - Private- / Corporate Loans	Loans & Deposits
	Collateral Administration
Core Banking - Card Management	Cards
	Payments
CRM - Customer Management / Customer Core Data	Servicing
	Customer Management
	Operational Services
CRM - Customer Scoring / Account Management / Customer Risk Management	Account Management
	Customer Management
CRM - Document Management	Document Management & Archive
CRM - Customer Services	Customer Services
	Corporate Financing & Advisory Services
Private Banking: Order & Portfolio Management / Risk Management	Market Operations
	Bank Portfolio & Treasury
Private Banking: Asset / Asset Liability Management	Bank Portfolio & Treasury
Private Banking: Market Data Modeling / Market Risk Management	Market Data
	Models
Private Banking: Trade & Investment	Trade Banking
	Investment Management
	Wholesale Trading

Table 2: Mapping of the application baseline blueprint against the BIAN Service Landscape

Compared to the service landscape of the BIAN, the CBS modules were split over several service domain clusters. For instance, the account current module is split over the product management, account management and the regulations & compliance service cluster due to the fact that its sub functions belong to these clusters. As a consequence, the resulting functional architecture of the transformed CBS business logic contains the following service domain clusters, according to the BIAN:

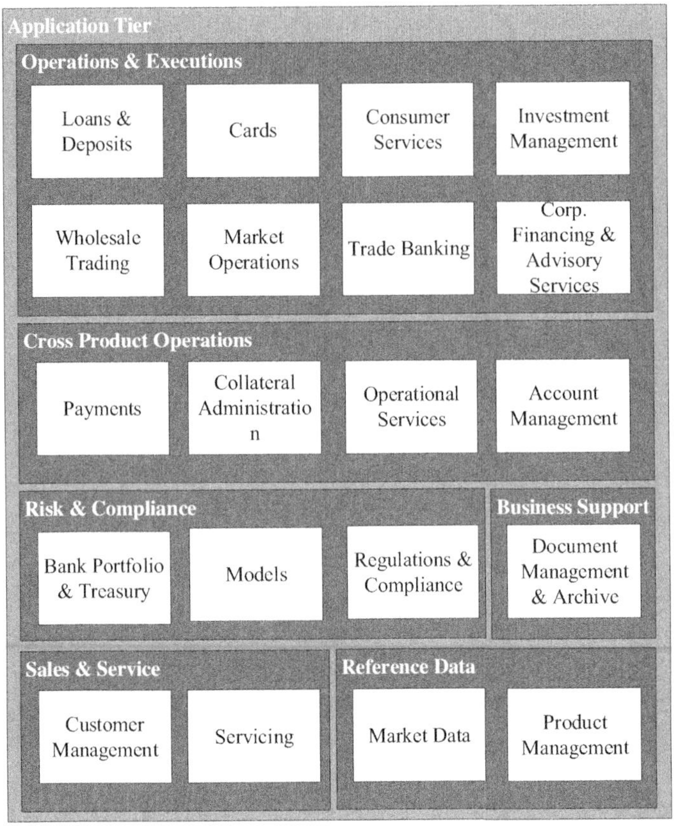

Illustration 21: Resulting Target Architecture after the Application of the BIAN

In connection with the technical specifications, the selected service domain clusters illustrate the target architecture. Obviously not all functions of the service domain clusters, specified in the BIAN standard, will be needed and the result must not absolutely comply 100% percent with the standard as every bank has its own specifics. Moreover, not every function of each listed cluster will be required, only the ones which are actually used by the organizational units are necessary. To ensure that no unneeded functions are implemented and no needed functionality is missing, the contained functions must be cross checked against the banks business service domains, that were raised in section 6.1.1. BIAN proposes, that this should be achieved through the use of value chains. However a simple check for each service domain on whether it is needed by at least one organizational unit is also a valid verification approach. In addition, all use cases of each business service domain also need to be covered by the target architecture of the CBS.

The result of the cross check should be a raw mapping of BIAN service domains to each business service domain (organizational unit) that is required, in order to fulfil its business processes. As a final step, the given (BIAN compliant) target architecture must be versioned as it describes the strategic architectural objective of the CBS and could be superseded by a subsequent version in the future.

6.1.4. Selection of modernization instruments

Once the target application has been fixed and versioned, it is necessary to select the modernization instrument for each component of the application baseline. As already mentioned, the following instruments are available:

- Reverse Engineering and Model Driven Development
- Architectural Replacement, either through re-implementing functionality or buying and customizing functionality via the acquisition of an off the shelf product.
- Architectural Refactoring through adapting existing code.
- And decommissioning functionality which will no longer be required after the modernization.

Regarding the selection of an appropriate modernization instrument, the technology, the architecture and the amount of lines of code of the existing source code plays a crucial role. Furthermore, the modernization should never be done without involving the software developers who are responsible for maintaining the existing code as they usually possess detailed knowledge about the code. If the existing source code is already written in the same language as specified in the target architecture and the required effort is reasonable, it may be an admissible approach to manually refactor the code until it fulfils the specification of the target. In the case that the legacy source code has a large amount of lines of code but is architecturally well structured, it would be possible to perform a semi-automated model driven transformation from the legacy language to the target language under the supervision of a developer who is familiar with the functionality. The code is in mainly transformed automatically, however this is done in parallel with regular testing and close verification in order to detect potential errors as soon as possible.
If the existing source code is considered to be too complex, grown too much or if there is simply no longer a developer available who is capable to maintain it, it is reasonable to think about its entire replacement through re-implementation or technological replacement. In terms of the exemplary Day-End processing routine, outlined in Appendix C, it consists out of a number of RPG IV Batchjobs which are run one after another on a daily basis. They usually entail a few of thousand lines of code and are closely interlinked to each other. Hence, it is feasible to either adapt or re-implement them consecutively or to transform them into the target language through a MDD based emulator (if possible). In terms of the entire exemplary CBS, as described in section 4.5, the overall approach would be to transform as many components as possible through model driven

development, especially the ones written in Java and C. If this is not possible for particular modules (e.g. the RPG IV modules), then they could either be re-implemented manually, or replaced through a more up-to-date frameworks that cover most Core Banking use cases.

6.1.5. Mapping of existing functionality to modernization instruments

After having selected the usable modernization methods, they need to be mapped to each module. The mapping is influenced by the:

- Complexity and structure of each module
- Knowledge about each module and available documentation
- Functional Size
- Analysability
- Estimated Cost
- Time effort
- And the estimated cost and transformability of the module

In that context, since the Day-End processing consists out of a number of batch jobs that are all sequentially executed one after another. All of them interact with their predecessor and successor job and while executing their logic, they also invoke further components (e.g. the calculation of interest rates) through defined interfaces. Each Batch job is therefore separable from other batch jobs through defined interfaces, which reduces the complexity of Day-End processing and allows the modernization of each Batch Job one by one. Under the assumption that the developers supporting the Day-End processing know its logic and functional mechanics, modernization based on Model Driven methods (e.g. an emulator who converts RPG code into the selected target language) is admissible in this case. As an alternative, re-implementing of the entire Day-End processing is admissible as well, but likely costlier as Day-End processing is a rather large component and tightly connected to Month-End and Year-End settlement functionality. Therefore, manual adaption or re-implementation are less appropriate than a model driven transformation. Hence, in this specific case, semi-automated model driven transformation (applying the emulator on the legacy code under the supervision of the supporting developers) is a feasible instrument to modernize the Day-End processing. The transformation can be done batch job by batch job with each resulting batch job being required to expose the same logical behaviour as its legacy counterpart and the interfaces for the communication to other batch jobs or components need to remain the same. As described in section 5.1.5, the decision about how to modernize this module should be taken by an expert team, consisting of developers and architects who are familiar with the legacy system.

6.1.6. Creation of a modernization strategy

After the modernization instrument has been selected for a specific module, its modernization needs to be coordinated with the other components undergoing a transformation. The advantage of Day-End processing is that the legacy system may remain in place until the modernized version has been sufficiently tested. Furthermore, its modularized sequential batch job property simplifies its transformation. Nevertheless, because of its number of dependencies and complex functionality, it should be scheduled into the final quarter of the overall modernization strategy. The advantage of this is, that the interfaces of other components which also went under transformation should already be modernized when Day-End processing begins to use them. Additionally, it is in general recommended to begin with the modernization of uncomplicated, but exemplary modules and proceed to the more complex ones afterwards. Hence, the precondition for Day-End processing is, that its required interfaces to other components are already modernized and tested properly. This precondition can be granulated to each individual batch-job contained in the Day-End processing. As post conditions (which may be granulated to each batch-job as well), the following would apply for the modernized Day-End processing:

- Each batch-job needs to comply with the target architecture.
- It needs to contain the (successfully tested) behaviour as stated in the point specifications and technical specifications of the target architecture.
- It should not be slower than the batch-job which it was modernized from.

Finally, each batch-job needs to be mapped to the originating batch-job in order to ensure traceability.

6.1.7. Creation of a PoC, Testing and PoC Extension

In the case where Day-End processing serves as a PoC component, this procedure can also be carried out step-by-step for each contained batch job where the first Batch-Job ("Execute Standing Orders") is the PoC itself and all sub sequent batch jobs are related to the PoC extension. This is feasible as Day-End processing has a large number of dependencies to other components but is internally separable. Furthermore, the execution of standing orders (payment) is not the easiest module, and through the model driven modernization approach, which was selected in the previous section, a parallel version of the legacy Day-End processing is created, which leaves it intact in case the PoC does not work.

By attempting to modernize it, technical and organizational learnings may be yielded which can be incorporated into the existing modernization strategy. For each transformed Batch-Job of the Day-End processing the following steps need to be done:

- It needs to be tested against the technical and point spec requirements of the target architecture.
- It needs to be verified whether it fulfils the architectural principles as given in the requirements.
- It needs to be regression tested against its legacy counterpart, in order to ensure that its business logic is the same (with the exception of required functional changes in the course of its transformation)
- Its internal behaviour needs to be verified through unit tests.
- It needs to be integration tested in order to ensure that it interacts with existing legacy components and other already transformed components as expected.

As soon as each transformed Batch-Job is successfully tested in a development and testing environment, it may be put to live operation and as soon as all Batch-Jobs of the Day-End processing have been successfully transformed the PoC extension phase is considered complete.

6.2. Expert Interviews

The expert interviews were conducted based on an interview guideline which is appended in Appendix A, and the interview transcripts are contained in Appendix B. The main challenge in terms of conducting these interviews was to find experts which have enough practical experience with the modernization of Core Banking Systems and are also capable of viewing the proposed technical modernization process on an architectural level. In other words, the requirements to a reviewing expert were the following:

- He or she has to be a software architect.
- He or she needs to work in the banking branch and there with a focus on Core Banking Systems.
- He or she needs to have practical experience with the modernisation of Core Banking Systems.

The interviews for each person lasted around one and 1,5 hours and were structured in three parts. The first part was the introduction into chapter 4.5, 5 and 6.1 of this thesis, and making sure that they understood the process. During this stage, some intuitive feedback was given and occurring questions were discussed on an ad-hoc basis with the help of conceptual delineations drawn on a sheet of paper. Afterwards, the questionnaire of the interview was worked through and discussed. The questions of the questionnaire were kept on a high level and hence the feedback of the experts is individual. In general, both experts had a positive opinion over the proposed process concept and they benchmarked it to their experience. They considered it as a consistent meta process model which has potential for further development.

During the explanation and discussion of the process concept, they also stated constructive remarks which are summarized below:

- In general, the relation of a bank and its IT landscape is not a unidirectional relation from bank to IT or vice versa, but a bidirectional one with interdependencies. The proposed process, as it is, assumes that the banking business solemnly governs the IT landscape. In reality, IT also constrains business and enables business due to technological influences and trends. Furthermore, the IT also has an influence on business processes due to technology and this should be considered in the process.
- The modernization process does not only modernize or transform the technological architecture of a CBS, but also the business processes and hence the business architecture of the supported organization (bank). Therefore, a distinction should be made in the process concept between business architecture and software architecture, especially as the BIAN as a standard is rather related to business processes.
- A proof of concept should not be done once for each modernization cycle but once for each modernization instrument in order to check whether the modernization instrument is really feasible under the political-, financial- and technological circumstances of a core banking system. Aside from that, a PoC should not only focus on one specific module, but on a specific business process which is technologically depicted within the CBS and will be modernized accordingly as well. The reason for this is that a module usually has technological and business dependencies on other modules within the same using business process. A further advantage of focusing on the modernization of business processes instead of single modules, is that interdependencies to other components, that need to be included into the modernization strategy, become visible. A PoC focused on business processes delivers not only technical learnings but also organizational learnings which need to be examined as well and could result in a general modernization schedule which is based on less assumptions.
- As soon as the technical and organizational learnings of the PoC were included into the modernization strategy, it should be refined accordingly and the final modernization of the CBS should then be procedurally summarized in a Rollout process step. That means, the proposed process concept should be extended through a rollout step after executing the PoC which will result in a modernized business processes.
- Another input was to evaluate how the proposed modernization process fits together with other development practices such as DevOps or Continuous Integration.
- A modernization cycle which is successfully completed can never be restarted again in the same scope, timeframe or architectural change as this is unrealistic. Instead, after

having completed a modernization cycle a new modernization cycle with new input parameters needs to be defined. The input parameters (such as timeframe, scope or the technical change) must reflect the changing requirements of the using organization. In general, the functional scope which is to be modernized as well as the timeframe need to be defined at the start of a modernization cycle.

- Modernization of a Core Banking system also implies the modernization of the business processes which utilize the CBS. Therefore, the organizational- and the technological modernization need to be aligned.
- It should be possible to revert to previous steps in a modernization cycle in order to serve changing requirements which come from the business during a modernization run.
- The process concept should consider that it is not always possible (due to financial and human resource constraints) to continuously modernize a CBS.
- After each process step within the process concept, security mechanisms should be defined and implemented in order to perform a reality check. This should reduce the risk of wrong decisions and subsequent misplanning.
- The entire modernization process concept should be complemented with a practical approach to divide existing monolithic CBS into components or modules. The main challenge is to divide the CBS at the right interfaces. In that regard, the criteria of where to segregate a system into modules needs to be defined. An approach would be to measure the extent of coupling through the number of invocations of an interface. The more transactions run from function A to function B via interface C, the more coupled they are. If there are comparably few transactions (or invocations) through a defined interface, then this interface could be a candidate for decoupling and would serve as a border to a functional module. Due the complexity of modularizing a CBS, this alone might require several attempts.
- In addition to examining the future organization of a bank (based on the assumption that a CBS shall reflect the organization of a bank and its related use cases) and also the strategic requirements of a bank should be considered in a target architecture. Examples include; non-functional requirements (e.g. in terms of transaction speed or the trend to outsource functionality) as well as functional requirements such as the ability to cover multiple distribution channels (online banking, staff channel, self-service terminals, ATMs) with the same backend functionality or the ability to offer 24 hour services to the customer. Furthermore, experiences of other CBS modernizations should also be taken into account.
- The target architecture needs to be coordinated and approved by the banking business, both as a requester and as an owner. However, it might be a challenge to get usable requirements and to justify the target architecture to the business. Another decision that has to be agreed upon is what functionality shall be covered centrally in the back office and

what functionality shall be decentralized in the branches. Also, the style of functional coupling (coupling vs. decoupling) is a strategic decision that needs to be aligned with the business.

- During the evaluation of the bank's organization it is not enough to simply raise its organizational structure and its use cases but it also needs to be elaborated to what extent the bank's organization is adaptable to the BIAN and whether a BIAN conform target architecture is the right way for the bank. A drawback of the BIAN is, that each bank has its own specifics which may not be covered by the BIAN and although the BIAN is generally a standard, it is not a non plus ultra in the banking business. Therefore, the process concept as proposed should not solemnly rely on the BIAN but should leave the decision of the standard to the using bank to define its target architecture based on its own specifics and requirements. BIAN as a standard may serve as a topological guideline to sort business processes but it is not state of the art due to its limited applicability.
- The elaboration of use cases of the bank shall not necessarily be guided through the bank's departments but rather orientated on its business processes as they reflect the needs of the bank to a wider extent than its organization.
- An entirely service oriented CBS is in reality not practicable due to performance issues and too much decoupling. Accordingly, a compromise of a CBS which consists out of medium sized functional modules is a better approach than a monolithic CBS or a fully service oriented CBS. These components are then individually testable and may be replaced with comparably low impact to other modules.
- In terms of CBS modernization, a long term method of thinking is required which must also be reflected in the proposed CBS. In that regard, technologies that are chosen as target technologies should have a longer life cycle than five years (e.g. Java).
- A top down approach, as propagated in the proposed modernization process, is not always a good solution as wrong overall estimations with severe consequences could be taken. If applicable, a bottom up approach might be more practical.
- If a functional component is chosen for a PoC, it is less risky to choose a small component than a large, complex one. In addition, it makes sense to keep the scope of a modernization simple to reduce dependencies in one modernization cycle and to change the implementing language in a subsequent one instead of doing both steps in one wash.
- The proposed modernization concept as it is, does not encounter changes in the requirements of a bank. Banks are subject to (rapidly) changing regulatory requirements and are obliged to comply with them. Therefore, changing requirements need to be coverable in a long term modernization run.

After the process concept was explained and discussed with both experts, both filled out the guideline questions with the questions varying in parts based on the situation. Their answers are summarized below.

1. **Overall Questions about the process:**
   a. Did you understand the process?
      The modernization process was easily understandable for both experts.
   b. What is your overall opinion on the process?
      For the first expert, the process concept was a great meta approach to govern modernization projects, however he also pointed out that each described process step needs to be specified in more detail. But nevertheless he perceived the process as consistent, repeatable and reasonable from a technical-, but also from a business perspective. For the second expert, the process concept was similar to a normal software development process. He stated that it is rather obvious that each software modernization needs to contain an analysis of the existing software and a definition of a target. He perceived the proposed process as an approach to solve problems but he was not sure whether the process, in its current state, is helpful on software engineering level.

2. **Feasibility:**
   a. Do you think that this process is feasible to existing CBS?
      For both experts the process is generally feasible. The first expert added that the layer below the given meta layer needs to be detailed much more and the second expert remarked that a proper modularization of the existing legacy CBS is a necessary precondition for the application of the given process concept. He also explained that aside from the technological and architectural modernization of a CBS, strategic goals (such as the ability to serve multiple distribution channels with the same functionality) also need to be addressed within the concept as well.
   b. If not, why?
      This question did not need to be answered as both experts considered the process to be feasible.

3. **Advantages / Shortfalls:**
   a. What risks do you see with the proposed modernization process? / What would you do different?
      For the first expert, it was important to have control mechanisms in the concept after each process step in order to avoid incorrect planning or wrong decisions with large

impacts on the system. The second expert stated that the concept is rather high level, which is in principle not problematic, but nevertheless each bank has its own specifics which might not be considered by a process concept as described. In addition, a target architecture needs to be aligned and approved by the business. Both experts had the same opinion that the concept needs to go into more detail in order to be usable in reality. Another point which was raised by the first expert, was that enough financial and human resources need to be available to conduct such a modernization cycle and the transformation needs to be supported by the governing banking business and must be aligned with the organization.

b. What strengths/shortfalls do you see in this modernization process?
   The first expert referred to the flexible usage and the open choice of granularity and scope as the main advantages. Furthermore, the ability to run this process in several parallel modernization cycles was also perceived as an advantage. On the other hand, the complexity of governing such a process (implied through its openness and flexibility) was recognized as a potential drawback. Aside from that, the process also suggests that an entire CBS might be modernized in one cycle which bears its risks as well.

7. Summary, Results and Outlook

7.1. Summary

In the course of this thesis, the topic of Core Banking Systems was outlined extensively in connection with architectural software modernization. First, the scientific advancements were examined and it became clear that modernization in connection with core banking systems is still a rather unexplored field from a scientific perspective, as it is a sub-discipline of software modernization in general. Instead, more practical oriented approaches had emerged especially from the banking industries as outdated but complex core banking systems hamper current strategical and technological banking trends more and more. Then the theoretical foundations of core banking systems were discussed including an attempt to formally define the term "Core Banking System" from a scientific point of view. Next, the historical development was shortly described and the main functions of a standard state of the art core banking system were outlined. These functions consist of:

- Management of Customer Core Data
- Electronic Funds Transfer
- Account Current
- Trade and Investment
- And Loans.

Subsequently, this thesis focused on software architectures in general and tried to define them, as well as depict the central elements of a software architecture. It outlined the 4+1 architectural view model of Kruchten [30] and explained the basic architectural styles, principles, and patterns. The previous descriptions of CBS and architectures were then the theoretical basis for chapter four, where CBS modernization was examined from a scientific- as well as an industrial oriented approach. First, general modernization approaches of software architecture were explained and it was discovered that both their methodological approaches and their foci are different from each other (e.g. architectural roadmaps vs. model-driven software modernization). Then, the BIAN [88], which provides a business process aligned industry standard for modern CBS architectures based on SOA, was examined. It contains a service landscape that enables banks and CBS vendors to develop their CBS towards a common standard which in turn aids interoperability and flexibility of CBS and shall reduce complexity. Next, the architectures of existing core banking systems were critically evaluated based on public sources. The CBS examined were Avaloq [80], Finnova [81], Temenos [82], Oracle Flexcube [89] and Infosys Finacle [90]. They were compared to each other and their individual weak points and strongpoints were outlined. The comparison and evaluation brought a practical industry-related aspect into this thesis and the learnings of the evaluation were then the basis for the subsequent modernization process. Then, an exemplary outdated CBS architecture was defined in high-level terms which were, on the one hand, realistic, and on the other hand technologically and architecturally heterogeneous. This case study served as example for the evaluation of the proposed modernization process in chapter five. The modernization process itself, as the scientific main result of this thesis, was then created based on the previously gathered knowledge. It consists of nine steps that may be executed recurringly, depending on the specific needs of a using CBS modernization project. The process is based on the assumption that a CBS shall always reflect a bank's organization and business processes. The steps of the modernization process are the following:

1. Assessment of existing Business Service Domains containing the following substeps:
    a. Elaboration of the organization of a bank.
    b. Elicitation of the business process model of the user bank.
    c. Incorporation of the future strategy of the using bank.
2. Assessment of the current CBS functionality, including the functional topology, its interfaces, the creation of an application baseline, and the assessment of the existing functionality against the bank's future business processes.
3. Creation of a Target Architecture which is aligned to BIAN including the creation of functional and non-functional requirements and the development of technical specifications in order to develop from the legacy functionality into a new functionality in the desired architecture and technology.
4. Definition of the available modernization instruments, which are either model-driven modernization, or reverse engineering, architectural replacement, refactoring and transformation or simply the decommissioning of unneeded functionality.
5. Mapping of the given modernization instruments to legacy modules, based on complexity, available knowledge, functional size, analysability, estimated modernization costs, time effort, and technology.
6. Creation of a time-based modernization strategy.
7. Creation of a Proof of Concept in order to demonstrate that the created modernization strategy is realistic and (regression) testing against the related legacy functionality and the given specifications.
8. Extending the PoC until the required target architecture is fully implemented.
9. Restarting the entire modernization cycle for the next modernization in the case that this is required or necessary.

The scientific evaluation of the proposed process was then carried out with the use of two approaches. First, it is applied against the exemplary outdated software architecture as depicted in chapter 4.5, and each process step is described in its application. Then, the process was critically evaluated via qualitative expert interviews with two experts who have practical experience with architectural software modernization in the context of core banking systems. With their help and experience, the proposed process was benchmarked against the reality and also in parts compared to other modernization processes that are individually adapted in each bank and vendor (if a modernization approach exists). The result and the learnings of the expert interviews are then gathered in chapter 6.2.

7.2. Scientific Results and added Value

One of the two main scientific results of this thesis is the theoretical description of Core Banking Systems in section 3.1. In this section, the functionality of CBS was outlined and in that regard, it answers the first research question of this thesis as given in section the first research question, as given in section 1.1.
The second main scientific result is the development of a process concept for the modernization of Core Banking Systems as described in chapter 5. It is the answer to the second research question, and outlines a recurring process, which takes the business architecture as well as the strategy of the using bank into account. In its design, it shall present a high-level guideline to the reader, how a CBS modernization can be conducted. The process itself is innovative and customized to the context of CBS and banks (at least according to current research no comparable CBS modernization process exists in publicly available literature). The process itself is an open framework, which has the following properties:

- It is a technology and architecture-independent top-down approach.
- It is flexible and consistent.
- It is open to customization, extendable and adaptable in its structure to the specific circumstances of a bank.
- It is adaptable in terms of the modernization scope and granularity
- It is recurrent and the actions within the process concept are traceable.
- It has a focus on processes, supports agility and offers an opportunity to engage in ongoing modernization.
- Furthermore, it may adopt different architectural modernization strategies.

In its current state, the process has been evaluated on a theoretical basis and has not yet been applied in practice. To be admissible in on a real CBS, it requires further specification on a more detailed level, incorporating the CBS' specifics. Furthermore, surrounding aspects like business support, resources, and financial aspects need to be clarified since they are vital for its successful execution. For instance, it needs to be complemented with consistent project management, and due to its flexibility it is prone to wrong decisions and it leaves a number of decisions open. Aside from the missing project management, the modernization process, in its current version, assumes that an existing CBS is already split up into proper modules. Hence, it does not cover the technical modularization of legacy CBS (which often have a monolithic architecture) into processible components, since this is already on its own a complex task.

The application of the developed process on the exemplary outdated CBS architecture (see section 4.5) showed that it is possible to modernize CBS with the given process. The process is capable of adapting to various specifics of a CBS and creates a basis in terms of scheduling for further work. Also during the interviews, both experts pointed out, that the process as given is a good start and usable in reality (after a sophisticated specification in more detail). More specifically, the process is a good meta layer in order to control and orchestrate a number of smaller modernization projects.

However, they also pointed out a number of fields for improvement that can be considered are a basis for further research and development:

- It should address the interactions between business architecture (business processes) and technology as the process currently assumes that IT is only driven by business and not vice versa. In this regard, it should either draw a demarcation line between software architecture and business architecture, or it should cover the transformation of a bank's business process as well. Furthermore, the process should also shift its focus from a bank's organizational structure to its business processes.
- The process needs to be extended with more security mechanisms in order to prevent wrong decisions. The process contains a PoC phase, but it is not enough to conduct one PoC for an entire modernization cycle, instead, a PoC should be done for each chosen modernization instrument. The subsequent findings then need to be addressed in a separate planning phase where the modernization strategy is enhanced by the (technical and organizational) learnings from the PoCs. Also, the scope of a PoC should not be an architectural module but rather a business process in order to gain more control over interdependencies to other processes.
- The process should be further developed by including a rollout process step and its target architecture needs to be coordinated with the banking business in order to address strategic decisions. Furthermore, the entire process of technical and organizational modernization needs to be done in accordance with the using business that will utilize the provided business processes.
- It needs to be able to encounter both changing and also larger strategic requirements from the bank. These requirements need to be elaborated, usable and understandable. Moreover, while the BIAN itself is an important standard to banks, they are not required to comply with the BIAN and usually have specifics that are not covered by the BIAN at all. Therefore, an improvement to the process would be to make it independent from the

BIAN in order to make it usable to banks that want to implement a target architecture under their specific topology.

7.3. Outlook

In a global context, the proposed modernization process is one approach in a number of methodologies. In general, banks who still utilize a mainframe-based CBS, or simply an outdated CBS are constantly challenged through their technological constraints that act as obstacles in the technological and strategic development of a bank. Especially as banking trends tend towards agility and flexibility, inflexible and outdated CBS are a problem. Hence, banks and CBS vendors face continuous strategic and business pressure to get their utilized CBS projects into an up to date shape. This problem is also exacerbated by the ongoing change in the generation of technologists, where older staff, who possess know-how about the outdated system retire or pass away. One way to tackle this issue, is to replace the outdated CBS by a new one, which is on the one hand, cost-intensive and on the other hand usually a large scale project with a recognizable amount of risk (e.g. if unsolvable technical problems occur). The other approach is to gradually modernize the existing CBS which may take more time than simply replacing it but is a much more transparent, controllable and less risky course of action.
In any case, modernization of CBS is still a young industrial field which is hardly (and only in diverging aspects) covered by science. But it is anticipated that this field will gain more and more importance in the banking and insurance branch in the upcoming years. And in that context, this thesis delivers a workable schematic approach for the modernization of the CBS architecture of an arbitrary bank.

References

A. Literature

[1] Aksit, M. (Ed.). (2012). Software architectures and component technology (Vol. 648). Springer Science & Business Media.

[2] Gomaa, H. (2011). Software modeling and design: UML, use cases, patterns, and software architectures. Cambridge University Press.

[3] Schmidt, D. C., Stal, M., Rohnert, H., & Buschmann, F. (2013). Pattern-Oriented Software Architecture, Patterns for Concurrent and Networked Objects (Vol. 2). John Wiley & Sons.

[4] Bernus, P., Mertins, K., & Schmidt, G. J. (Eds.). (2013). Handbook on architectures of information systems. Springer Science & Business Media.

[5] Scheer, A. W. (2013). Architektur integrierter Informationssysteme: Grundlagen der Unternehmensmodellierung. Springer-Verlag.

[6] Moto-Oka, T. (Ed.). (2012). Fifth Generation Computer Systems. Amsterdam. North-Holland.

[7] Kroenke, D. (2013). MIS essentials. Prentice Hall Press, Upper Saddle River.

[8] Pawlak, Z. (1981). Information systems theoretical foundations. Information systems, 6(3), 205-218.

[9] Wood-Harper, A. T., Antill, L., & Avison, D. E. (1985). Information systems definition: the Multiview approach.

[10] Izquierdo, J. L. C., & Molina, J. G. (2009). A domain specific language for extracting models in software modernization. In Model Driven Architecture-Foundations and Applications (pp. 82-97). Springer Berlin Heidelberg.

[11] Van Hoorn, A., Frey, S., Goerigk, W., Hasselbring, W., Knoche, H., Köster, S., ... & Wittmüss, N. (2011). DynaMod project: Dynamic analysis for model-driven software modernization.

[12] Newcomb, P. (2005, November). Architecture-driven modernization (ADM). In Reverse Engineering, 12th Working Conference on (pp. 237-237). IEEE.

[13] Sadovykh, A., Vigier, L., Hoffmann, A., Grossmann, J., Ritter, T., Gomez, E., & Estekhin, O. (2009, June). Architecture driven modernization in practice–study results. In Engineering of Complex Computer Systems, 2009 14th IEEE International Conference on (pp. 50-57). IEEE.

[14] Ulrich, W. M., & Newcomb, P. (2010). Information systems transformation: architecture-driven modernization case studies. Morgan Kaufmann.

[15] Zimmermann, O., Milinski, S., Craes, M., & Oellermann, F. (2004, October). Second generation web services-oriented architecture in production in the finance industry. In Companion to the 19th annual ACM SIGPLAN conference on Object-oriented programming systems, languages, and applications (pp. 283-289). ACM.

[16] Baskerville, R., Cavallari, M., Hjort-Madsen, K., Pries-Heje, J., Sorrentino, M., & Virili, F. (2005). Extensible architectures: the strategic value of service oriented architecture in banking. ECIS 2005 Proceedings, 61.

[17] Kilimnik, J., & Pavlovski, C. (2014, July). Core Banking Modernization. In the 9th International Conference on Information Technology and Applications (ICITA).

[18] Liu, R., Wu, F., Patnaik, Y., & Kumaran, S. (2009, September). Business entities: An SOA approach to progressive core banking renovation. In Services Computing, 2009. SCC'09. IEEE International Conference on (pp. 466-473). IEEE.

[19] Hussain, S. J., Kumar, M., & Hussain, S. J. (2006, November). Meta architecture to support layered banking systems. In Emerging Technologies, 2006. ICET'06. International Conference on (pp. 754-760). IEEE.

[20] Maier, M. W., Emery, D., & Hilliard, R. (2004). ANSI/IEEE 1471 and systems engineering. Systems Engineering, 7(3), 257-270.

[21] Dustdar, S., Gall, H., & Hauswirth, M. (2013). Software-architekturen für verteilte Systeme: Prinzipien, Bausteine und Standardarchitekturen für moderne Software. Springer-Verlag.

[22] Kazman, R., Klein, M., Barbacci, M., Longstaff, T., Lipson, H., & Carriere, J. (1998, August). The architecture tradeoff analysis method. In Engineering of Complex Computer Systems, 1998. ICECCS'98. Proceedings. Fourth IEEE International Conference on (pp. 68-78). IEEE.

[23] Tekinerdogan, B. (2004, June). ASAAM: Aspectual software architecture analysis method. In Software Architecture, 2004. WICSA 2004. Proceedings. Fourth Working IEEE/IFIP Conference on (pp. 5-14). IEEE.

[24] Kazman, R., Bass, L., Webb, M., & Abowd, G. (1994, May). SAAM: A method for analyzing the properties of software architectures. In Proceedings of the 16th international conference on Software engineering (pp. 81-90). IEEE Computer Society Press.

[25] Kazman, R., Bass, L., Klein, M., Lattanze, T., & Northrop, L. (2005). A basis for analyzing software architecture analysis methods. Software Quality Journal, 13(4), 329-355.

[26] Babar, M. A., & Gorton, I. (2009). Software architecture review: The state of practice. Computer, (7), 26-32.

[27] Abowd, G., Bass, L., Clements, P., Kazman, R., & Northrop, L. (1997). Recommended Best Industrial Practice for Software Architecture Evaluation (No. CMU/SEI-96-TR-025). Carnegie-Mellon University Pittsburgh PA Software Engineering Inst.

[28] Clements, P. C. (2000). Active reviews for intermediate designs (No. CMU/SEI-2000-TN-009). CARNEGIE-MELLON UNIV PITTSBURGH PA SOFTWARE ENGINEERING INST.

[29] Clements, P., Kazman, R., & Klein, M. (2003). Evaluating software architectures. 清华大学出版社.

[30] Kruchten, P. B. (1995). The 4+1 view model of architecture. Software, IEEE, 12(6), 42-50.

[31] Demir, K. A. (2015). Multi-View Software Architecture Design: Case Study of a Mission-Critical Defense System. Computer and Information Science, 8(4), p12.

[32] Reekie, F., & McCarthy, T. (1995). Reekie's architectural drawing. Architectural Press.

[33] Shaw, M., & Garlan, D. (1996). Software architecture: perspectives on an emerging discipline (Vol. 1, p. 12). Englewood Cliffs: Prentice Hall.

[34] Ernst, N. A., Popeck, M., Bachmann, F., & Donohoe, P. (2016, April). Creating Software Modernization Roadmaps: The Architecture Options Workshop. In Software Architecture (WICSA), 2016 13th Working IEEE/IFIP Conference on (pp. 71-80). IEEE.

[35] Danisewicz, P., McGowan, D., Onali, E., & Schaeck, K. (2018). The real effects of banking supervision: Evidence from enforcement actions. Journal of Financial Intermediation, 35, 86-101.

[36] Aakash Ahmad, Pooyan Jamshidi, and Claus Pahl. 2013. A framework for acquisition and application of software architecture evolution knowledge: 14. SIGSOFT Softw. Eng. Notes 38, 5 (August 2013), 1-7. DOI=10.1145/2507288.2507301 http://doi.acm.org/10.1145/2507288.2507301

[37] Fuentes-Fernández, R., Pavón, J., & Garijo, F. (2012). A model-driven process for the modernization of component-based systems. Science of Computer Programming, 77(3), 247-269.

[38] Plakidas, K., Schall, D., & Zdun, U. (2018, September). Software Migration and Architecture Evolution with Industrial Platforms: A Multi-Case Study. In European Conference on Software Architecture (pp. 336-343). Springer, Cham.

[39] Plakidas, K., Schall, D., & Zdun, U. (2018). Model-based support for decision-making in architecture evolution of complex software systems.

[40] Knoche, H., & Hasselbring, W. (2018). Using Microservices for Legacy Software Modernization. IEEE Software, 35(3), 44-49.

[41] Mili, H., El Boussaidi, G., Shatnawi, A., Guéhéneuc, Y. G., Moha, N., Privat, J., & Valtchev, P. (2017). Service-oriented re-engineering of legacy JEE applications: Issues and research directions.

[42] Jamshidi, P., Pahl, C., & Mendonça, N. C. (2017). Pattern-based multi-cloud architecture migration. Software: Practice and Experience, 47(9), 1159-1184.

[43] Jamshidi, P., Pahl, C., Mendonça, N. C., Lewis, J., & Tilkov, S. (2018). Microservices: The Journey So Far and Challenges Ahead. IEEE Software, 35(3), 24-35.

[44] Fowley, F., Elango, D. M., Magar, H., & Pahl, C. (2017, January). Software system migration to cloud-native architectures for SME-sized software vendors. In International Conference on Current Trends in Theory and Practice of Informatics (pp. 498-509). Springer, Cham.

[45] Favre, L. M., Martinez, L., & Pereira, C. T. (2018). Model-Driven Software Modernization. In Encyclopedia of Information Science and Technology, Fourth Edition (pp. 7447-7458). IGI Global.

[46] Brambilla, M., Cabot, J., & Wimmer, M. (2017). Model-driven software engineering in practice. Synthesis Lectures on Software Engineering, 3(1), 1-207.

[47] Jamshidi, P., Ghafari, M., Ahmad, A., & Pahl, C. (2013). A framework for classifying and comparing architecture-centric software evolution research.

[48] Fuentes-Fernández, R., Pavón, J., & Garijo, F. (2012). A model-driven process for the modernization of component-based systems. Science of Computer Programming, 77(3), 247-269.

[49] Menychtas, A., Santzaridou, C., Kousiouris, G., Varvarigou, T., Orue-Echevarria, L., Alonso, J., ... & Pellens, B. (2013, September). ARTIST Methodology and Framework: A novel approach for the migration of legacy software on the Cloud. In 2nd Workshop on Management of resources and services In Cloud And Sky computing (MICAS 2013).

[50] Johanson, A., & Hasselbring, W. (2018). Software Engineering for Computational Science: Past, Present, Future. Computing in Science & Engineering.

[51] Stair, R., & Reynolds, G. (2017). Fundamentals of information systems. Cengage Learning.

[52] Chorafas, D. N. (2016). Enterprise architecture and new generation information systems. CRC Press.

[53] Hariharan, N. P., & Reeshma, K. J. (2015). Challenges of core banking systems. Mediterranean Journal of Social Sciences, 6(5), 24.

[54] Fernando, S. D. (2015). Core Banking Systems and Business Intelligence for Effective Strategic Decision Making.

[55] Gasser, U., Gassmann, O., Hens, T., Leifer, L., Puschmann, T., & Zhao, L. (2017). Digital Banking 2025.

[56] Bass, L., Clements, P., & Kazman, R. (2003). Software architecture in practice. Addison-Wesley Professional.

[57] Rozanski, N., & Woods, E. (2012). Software systems architecture: working with stakeholders using viewpoints and perspectives. Addison-Wesley.

[58] Galster, M., Weyns, D., Avgeriou, P., & Becker, M. (2013). Variability in software architecture: views and beyond. Software Engineering Notes: an Informal Newsletter of The Specia, 38(1), 46-49.

[59] Schmidt, D. C., Stal, M., Rohnert, H., & Buschmann, F. (2013). Pattern-Oriented Software Architecture, Patterns for Concurrent and Networked Objects (Vol. 2). John Wiley & Sons.

[60] Gomaa, H., Hashimoto, K., Kim, M., Malek, S., & Menascé, D. A. (2010, March). Software adaptation patterns for service-oriented architectures. In Proceedings of the 2010 ACM Symposium on Applied Computing (pp. 462-469). ACM.

[61] Smith, J. M. (2012). Elemental design patterns. Addison-Wesley Professional.

[62] Koziolek, H. (2011, June). Sustainability evaluation of software architectures: a systematic review. In Proceedings of the joint ACM SIGSOFT conference--QoSA and ACM SIGSOFT symposium--ISARCS on Quality of software architectures--QoSA and architecting critical systems--ISARCS (pp. 3-12). ACM.

[63] Breivold, H. P., Crnkovic, I., & Larsson, M. (2012). A systematic review of software architecture evolution research. Information and Software Technology, 54(1), 16-40.

[64] Kim, J. S., & Garlan, D. (2010). Analyzing architectural styles. Journal of Systems and Software, 83(7), 1216-1235.

[65] Sharma, A., Kumar, M., & Agarwal, S. (2015). A complete survey on software architectural styles and patterns. Procedia Computer Science, 70, 16-28.

[66] Ghafari, H., & Ansari, S. (2018). Effect of five key factors on the implementation of core banking system. International Journal of Scientific Research and Management, 6(07).

[67] Schü, J., Saßmann, K., Gottschalk, M. Core Banking Criteria. (2015). Powerpoint Presentation.

[68] Kotarba, M. (2016). New factors inducing changes in the retail banking customer relationship management (CRM) and their exploration by the FinTech industry. Foundations of management, 8(1), 69-78.

[69] Sherif, M. H. (2016). Protocols for secure electronic commerce. CRC press.

[70] Shelton, D., & Sharma, S. (2016). Electronic Delivery of Wages, Salaries, Reimbursements, and Refunds. Policy, 6, 9.

[71] Rusu, C., & Stix, H. (2017). Cash and card payments–recent results of the Austrian payment diary survey. Monetary Policy and the Economy Q, 1, 19-31.

[72] Schuh, S. D., & Stavins, J. (2011). How consumers pay: adoption and use of payments.

[73] Freixas, X., & Rochet, J. C. (2008). Microeconomics of banking. MIT press.

[74] Mattoo, A., Stern, R. M., & Zanini, G. (Eds.). (2007). A handbook of international trade in services. The World Bank.

[75] Hwang, K., & Jotwani, N. (2016). Advanced Computer Architecture, 3e. McGraw-Hill Education.

[76] Smith, J. E., & Nair, R. (2004). An overview of virtual machine architectures. Virtual Machines: Architectures, Implementations and Applications. Morgan-Kaufmann.

[77] Hamdaqa, M., & Tahvildari, L. (2014, November). The (5+ 1) architectural view model for cloud applications. In Proceedings of 24th Annual International Conference on Computer Science and Software Engineering (pp. 46-60). IBM Corp..

B. Weblinks

[78] Webpage of the ModelCVS project: Retrieved from http://www.modelcvs.org/index.html (October 5th, 2018).

[79] Webpage of the aim42 modernization approach: Retrieved from http://aim42.org/ (October 5th, 2018).

[80] Web presence of Avaloq: Retrieved from https://www.avaloq.com/de/ (October 5th, 2019).

[81] Web presence of Finnova: Retrieved from http://www.finnova.com/de/home-de.html (October 5th, 2019).

[82] Web presence of Temenos: Retrieved from http://www.temenos.com/en/ (October 5th, 2019).

[83] Gartner's definition of Core Banking Systems: Retrieved from http://www.gartner.com/it-glossary/core-banking-systems/ (October 5th, 2019).

[84] CBS history in India: Retrieved from http://thebankingsystem.blogspot.co.at /2009/08/history-of-core-banking-ystem-in-india.html (October 5th, 2019).

[85] Bank Tiers: Retrieved from http://www.gartner.com/it-glossary/bank-tier/ (October 5th, 2019).

[86] Data centered Architecture: Retrieved from http://www.tutorialspoint.com/software_architecture_design/data_centered_architecture.htm (October 5th, 2019).

[87] Pipes: Retrieved from http://www.westwind.com/reference/os-x/commandline/ pipes.html (October 5th, 2019).

[88] The BIAN service landscape: Retrieved from https://bian.org/servicelandscape/ (October 5th, 2019).

[89] Web Presence of Oracle Flexcube: Retrieved from http://www.oracle.com/us/products/applications/financial-services/flexcube/index.html (October 5th, 2019).

[90] Web Presence of Fincale: Retrieved from https://www.edgeverve.com/finacle/ (October 5th, 2019).

[91] The BIAN How to Guide in Version 7.0: https://bian.org/deliverables/bian-how-to-guide/ (October 5th, 2019).

[92] Miller, Cody, Technological Evolution in Software Engineering (2018). Engineering and Technology Management Student Projects. 2239. https://pdxscholar.library.pdx.edu/etm_studentprojects/2239 (October 5th, 2019).

[93] Heidmann, M. (2010). Overhauling banks' IT systems. McKinsey Quarterly, McKinsey & Company. https://www.mckinsey.com/business-functions/mckinsey-digital/our-insights/overhauling-banks-it-systems (October 5th, 2019).

[94] Web Presence of SWIFT: Retrieved from https://www2.swift.com/knowledgecentre/productcategory#Standards (October 5th, 2019).

[95] Web Presence of the BIAN: Retrieved from http://www.bian.org/ (October 5th, 2018).

[96] The ISO/IEC 25010 norm in version 2011: Retrieved from: https://www.iso.org/standard/35733.html (October 6th, 2019)

[97] Web Presence of MySQL: Retrieved from https://www.mysql.com (October 6th, 2019)

[98] Web Presence of PostgreSQL: Retrieved from https://www.postgresql.org/ (October 6th, 2019)

[99] Web Presence of Oracle's database branch: Retrieved from https://www.oracle.com/database/ (October 6th, 2019)

[100] Web Presence of IBM: Retrieved from www.ibm.com (October 6th, 2019)

[101] RPG Tutorial of IBM (RPG Café): Retrieved from https://www.ibm.com/developerworks/community/wikis/home?lang=en#!/wiki/We13116a562db_467e_bcd4_882013aec57a/page/Coding%20in%20RPG%20IV%20-%20a%20beginner's%20tutorial (October 6th, 2019)

[102] Lattice RPG Documentation: Retrieved from http://www.edm2.com/index.php/Lattice_RPG_II (October 6th, 2019)

[103] TPC/IP Tutorial as defined in IEEE RFC 1180: Retrieved from https://tools.ietf.org/html/rfc1180 (October 6th, 2019)

[104] The SQL specification as defined in ISO/IEC 9075-1 in version 2011: Retrieved from https://webstore.ansi.org/Standards/ISO/ISOIEC90752011 (October 6th, 2019)

[105] The Java language and Virtual Machine Specifications: Retrieved from https://docs.oracle.com/javase/specs/ (October 6th, 2019)

[106] Web Presence of Apache Ant: Retrieved from https://ant.apache.org/ (October 6th, 2019)

[107] Comparison of current OR Mapper Frameworks: Retrieved from http://www.ormeter.net (October 6th, 2019)

[108] PL/SQL specification of Oracle: Retrieved from https://www.oracletutorial.com/plsql-tutorial/plsql-package-specification/ (October 6th, 2019)

[109] GNU Tutorial on the creation of Unix makefiles: Retrieved from https://www.gnu.org/software/make/manual/make.html (October 6th, 2019)

[110] Description of the Oracle Enterprise Service Bus: Retrieved from https://www.oracle.com/technical-resources/articles/middleware/soa-ind-soa-esb.html (October 6th, 2019)

[111] The Open Group Unix Specification: Retrieved from https://publications.opengroup.org/t101?_ga=2.90703706.1342406596.1570364352-1751779014.1570364352 (October 6th, 2019)

[112] Extensible Markup Language (XML) specification in Version 5: Retrieved from https://www.w3.org/TR/xml/ (October 6th, 2019)

[113] The ISO/IEC 9899:2018 norm defining the C programming language in its current version: Retrieved from https://webstore.iec.ch/publication/63478 (October 6th, 2019)

[114] The Java Native Interface specification: Retrieved from https://docs.oracle.com/javase/7/docs/technotes/guides/jni/spec/jniTOC.html (October 6th, 2019)

[115] The Simple Object Access Protocol Standard in Version 1.2, presented by W3C: Retrieved from https://www.w3.org/TR/soap/ (October 6th, 2019)

[116] The Hypertext Transfer Protocol as defined in RFC 7540: Retrieved from https://tools.ietf.org/html/rfc7540 (October 6th, 2019)

[117] The Official Web Presence of JavaScript: Retrieved from https://www.javascript.com/ (October 6th, 2019)

[118] Web Presence of AngularJS: Retrieved from https://angularjs.org/ (October 6th, 2019)

[119] The Secure Sockets Layer RFC in Version 3.0: Retrieved from https://tools.ietf.org/html/rfc6101 (October 6th, 2019)

[120] Web Presence of the Apache Tomcat Server: Retrieved from http://tomcat.apache.org/ (October 6th, 2019)

[121] Web Presence of Java RMI, by Oracle: Retrieved from https://docs.oracle.com/javase/tutorial/rmi/ (October 6th, 2019)

[122] Blog Entry of Mátyás Lancelot Bors describing architectural patterns: Retrieved from https://medium.com/@mlbors/architectural-styles-and-architectural-patterns-c240f7df88a0 (October 6th, 2019)

[123] Common architectural patterns: Retrieved from https://towardsdatascience.com/10-common-software-architectural-patterns-in-a-nutshell-a0b47a1e9013 (October 6th, 2019)

Appendix

A. Expert Interview

The following content outlines the structure of the expert interviews:

Introduction

Thank you very much for giving me the opportunity to do this interview with you. I am currently writing on my master thesis with the topic "Deduction of a Technical Modernization Process for the Software Architecture of Core Banking Systems". In the course of this thesis I developed a high level modernization process and I would like to do a number of expert interviews in order to evaluate the given process through experts with substantial practical experience in the field of Core Banking Systems. The motivation of this thesis are numerous core banking projects which are confronted with outdated yet hard to modernize technologies within their functional cores. The given process shall offer a guideline which allows CBS vendors to modernize their systems in a coordinated way and is technology and vendor independent as well as adaptable to any preexisting architecture. Furthermore, in its current version it orientates to the BIAN (Banking Industries Architecture Network) as a standard target architecture for Core Banking Systems.

The Interview will take approximately 120 Minutes where every participant will be given the same set of questions. In the course of the interview, an audio recorder will record the answers, which will be subsequently transcribed into written form. The audio recordings will not be published in any way.

The interview is structured as follows:

1. Reading of chapter 4.5, 5 and 6.1 of the master thesis in order to understand the proposed modernization process as well as the application of the exemplary architecture on the process.
2. Discussion of occurring questions, based on the reading.
3. Working through the interview questions:
    a. Overall questions about the process.
    b. The process versus the Core Banking System of the expert.
    c. Feasibility

Interview Questions:

1. **Overall Questions about the process:**
    a. Did you understand the process?
    b. What is your overall opinion on the process?

2. **Feasibility:**
    a. Do you think that this process is feasible to existing CBS?
    b. If not, why?

3. **Advantages / Shortfalls:**
    a. What risks do you see with the proposed modernization process?
    b. What would you do different?
    c. What strengths do you see in this modernization process?

Thank you very much for your time!

B. Interview Transcripts

The following interview transcriptions were done in two separate interview sessions with Software Architects who have decades of practical experience in the area of Core Banking Systems. Their statements are marked as "E" (Expert) and the questions and statements of the interviewer, Alexander Gruber, are marked as "I" (Interviewer). Both Interviews were conducted in German as the interviewer as well as the experts are all Austrians.

B.1. Interview 1

Interview between Alexander Gruber and the first expert on March 13th, 2018.

Kontext: Erklärung des exemplarischen Kernbanksystems an den Experten:

I: Also die übergreifenden Dinge, die nicht direkt das Kernbanksystem verwenden, hab ich mal rausgelassen.

E: Das meine ich nicht, es gibt allgemeine Funktionen die von allen Komponenten verwendet werden.

I: Achso, naja die sind schon drin.

E: Das heißt es gibt keine 1:1 Verdrahtung zwischen Funktion und Bereich, sondern eine Mehrfachverdrahtung zwischen verwendender Abteilung und Funktionsmodul.

I: Genau. Voraussetzung ist nur dass jedes Modul von mindestens einer Organisatorischen Einheit einer Bank verwendet werden muss.
E: Logisch, sonst macht es keinen Sinn. D.h. beispielsweise Treasury verwendet nicht nur treasuryspezifische Module sondern auch allgemeine.
I: Genau, und das Ganze system ist serviceorientiert und konform zum BIAN. ... (Weiter mit der Erklärung des vorgeschlagenen Modernisiserungsprozesses) Zuerst schaue ich mir an, welche Firmentopologie bzw. Organisation ich habe, und vor allem welche Firmenorganisation möchte ich in Zukunft haben? D.h. es wird bereits die organisatorische Zukunftsvision der Bank in das zu modernisierende Kernbanksystem einbezogen, inkl. der geplanten Business Schwerpunkte.
E: D.h. IST und Zukunft werden miteinbezogen, d.h. die Bank muss ihre Zukunftsszenarien bereits wissen.
I: Genau. Und mit diesem Prozess soll das Kernbanksystem nicht nur technologisch modernisiert werden sondern auch in seiner Funktionalität an die Strategie der Bank angepasst werden.
E: D.h. es gibt auch eine Transformation der Prozesse und der Organisation und nicht nur des Kernbanksystems.
I: Genau. Und ich schaue dann auch wo die Gaps zwischen bestehender Funktionalität und benötigter Funktionalität in der Zukunft sind. Und dabei schau ich zuerst, welche Funktionalität ich gerade im bestehenden Kernbanksystem habe. Wobei hier ist die größte Herausforderung das bestehende Kernbanksystem aufzumodulieren, d.h. Grenzen zwischen den Funktionen zu ziehen. Sowie ich das habe, erzeuge ich eine Target Architecture, die dem BIAN entspricht, und das mache ich in drei Schritten. Zuerst muss ich mir aus der BIAN service landscape heraussuchen welche Service Cluster Domains ich brauch. Aus diesen such ich mir dann die entsprechenden Service Domains raus. Danach mach ich ein Mapping der bestehenden Funktionalität auf diese Service Domains und sowie ich das dann hab, erzeuge ich dazu Spezifikationen, d.h. wie komme ich technisch von meiner bestehenden Funktionalität auf das gewünschte serviceorientierte Ziel?
E: Wo befindet sich dann der neue Businessprozess der daraus resultieren müsste? D.h. wo fließt dieser dann ein?
I: In der Target Architecture.
E: D.h. der neue Business Prozess fließt in die Target Architecture mit ein?
I: Genau.
E: Und das meiste an der Tranformation spielt sich dann eigentlich im Application Tier ab oder?
I: Genau, also eigentlich so ziemlich alles, wobei in meinem exemplarischen Fall ist das Kernbanksystem wirklich ein zusammengeflicktes System mit großen Modulen, wie man es in der Realität immer wieder sieht. Und diese Module muss ich dann auf den BIAN mappen, also auf die Service Domain Clusters vom BIAN. Das ist natürlich nicht immer 1:1, sondern de facto ein Mesh. Sowie ich das Mapping dann gemacht hab, muss ich mir pro Modul überlegen wie ich es modernisieren kann.
(Kurze Interviewpause)

E: Ok, aber was hast du dann? Du hast dann den IST Stand gemappt auf den BIAN und die Gaps die du für dein zukünftiges modernisisertes Kernbanksystem brauchst oder? D.h. beides müsste dann das Outcome der Target Architecture sein.
I: Genau. D.h. Summa Summarum schaue ich mir zuerst meine existierende Funktionalität an und erzeuge daraus eine Baseline of Applications (IST Stand). Und dann schau ich, wie sehr mein IST Stand der Target Architecture entspricht, und vor allem wo die Gaps sind. Danach gehe ich weiter und versionier das, weil das Ganze ein wiederkehrender Prozess ist. Weil theoretisch sollte Modernisierung nie aufhören sondern langfristig wiederkehrend sein. Nachdem ich die Baseline of Applications und die Target Architecture habe. muss ich mir in Spezifikationen anschauen wie ich vom IST Stand auf den SOLL Stand komm. Der BIAN definiert nämlich nur die Service Domains, spezifiziert sie allerdings nicht funktional aus. Dafür muss man aber nicht komplett dem BIAN entsprechen, da die meisten Banken auch noch ihre eigenen Anforderungen haben. Die Target Architecture muss ich weiters auch versionieren, da diese irgendwann im Idealfall die Basline of Applications im nächsten Modernisierungslauf wird. Sobald die Versionierung gemacht ist, muss ich mir jedes Modul einzeln, nach dem Divide and Conquer Ansatz ansehen, wobei hier zugegeben die Modularisierung nicht im Scope dieser Diplomarbeit ist, da das wieder eine DA für sich wäre. Für jedes Modul wird dann ein Modernisierungsinstrument wie Model Driven Development, Architectural Replacement o.Ä. gewählt.
E: Was noch fehlt ist das effektive Abschalten, weil es manchmal im IST Stand Dinge gibt, die man abschalten könnte.
I: Das hab ich auch, decommissioning. Also Summa Sumamrum soll die Summe aller Funktionen die Summe aller Anwendungsfälle der Bank abdecken.
E: Genau das ist der ideale Fall. Der ideale Fall ist immer, dass die Bank weis was sie tut, oft gibt es aber zwischen Bank und IT eine Wechselwirkung. Nicht immer kann die Bank das tun was sie will, weil es technisch nicht möglich ist und umgekehrt. D.h. es gibt immer eine Wechselwirkung zwischen Strategie und Implementierung. Das wär etwas das du hier noch einbauen solltest, da du hier von dem Fall ausgehst dass das Business die IT vor sich hertreibt, allerdings ist das nicht immer der Fall, da die Bank auch aus strategischen Entscheidungen heraus IT Komponenten ersetzt (z.B. Erste Bank netbanking wurde durch George ersetzt, weil netbanking nicht in der Lage war die strategischen Ziele der Bank zu erfüllen). Die IT treibt auch Business Prozesse vor sich her, bzw. verhindert auch Dinge.
I: Ich hab auch gehört dass der BIAN nicht immer so toll ist, da er verlangt dass die Bank ihre Organisation ändert, was die Bank in der Regel nicht machen wird und die Bank fragt dann wer das zahlen soll? Auf der anderen Seite kann die Bank mehr Dinge von der IT verlangen und nicht umgekehrt.
(Zurück zum Thema) Sowie ich meine Modernisierungsintrumente habe, und diese auch allen Komponenten zugeordnet hab, mach ich mir einen Zeitplan der besagt, wann und in welcher Reihenfolge welches Modul anhand seines gewählten Modernisierungsinstruments modernisiert

wird. Dieser Zeitplan ist auch abhängig von Technologien, Priorität, und den äußeren Rahmenumständen auf denen das Modernisierungsprojekt aufgebaut ist. Sowie ich den Zeitplan dann habe, nehme ich mir ein Modul und mache einen Proof of Concept. Das wird dann in ein transfomriertes Service umgesetzt.

E: Was ist der Benefit vom PoC?

I: Ich kann meine Findings vom PoC in die Modernisierungsstrategie wieder einbauen und kann die so verbessern.

E: Brauchst du nicht einen PoC pro Modernisierungsinstrument?

I: Ja, stimmt also pro ausgewähltem Instrument.

E: Vor allem dadurch, dass das Ganze eine Wechselwirkung zum Business Prozess hat, solltest du nicht nur ein Modul sondern einen ganzen Business Prozess als PoC modernisieren. Dadurch erkennst du nämlich auch Wechselwirkungen nach außen hin und kannst diese ebenfalls in die Modernisierungsstrategie einbauen für die Gesamtbank. Der PoC ist nämlich nicht nur technisch sondern hat auch Einfluss auf die Organisation und das sollte auch betrachtet werden. Weil so gesehen hättest du dann nämlich nach dem PoC nicht nur die technischen Learnings aus dem PoC, sondern auch die organisatorischen und daraus könntest du dann einen Gesamtplan bauen, der weniger auf Annahmen basiert.

I: Ok, danach sag ich testen. D.h. die transformierte Funktionalität muss der Ursprungsfunktionalität entsprechen, nur halt in einer anderen Architektur.

E: Oder mehr, oder anders. Weil technisch heißt nicht nur technisch, sondern auch funktional.

I: Bzw. die Funktionalität muss den Specs entsprechen. Sowie ich das dann gemacht hab, bau ich meinen Proof of Concept aus.

E: D.h. du würdest eine zweite Runde eines PoC machen?

I: Nein, ich würd den PoC gemäß der Modernisierungsstrategie solange ausweiten, bis alles modernisiert ist.

E: Ok, aber da fehlt noch was, du musst die Learnings in die Modernisierungsstrategie einbauen, du kannst nicht einfach davon ausgehen, dass der PoC ohne Probleme vonstatten geht und dass man kein Replanning machen muss. Ich würde an deiner Stelle ein eigenes Kapitel „Replanning" einbauen wo auch die Wechselwirkungen beschrieben sind und danach einen „Rollout" einbauen, mit dem einzelne Komponenten dann modernisiert ausgegeben werden.

I: Ok, danach extende ich meinen PoC (Rollout) und das wärs dann im Großen und Ganzen bereits

E: Stimmt und danach kannst du dann entscheiden, ob du danach nochmal eine Modernisierung machst.

I: Genau, die Grundidee ist dass eine Modernisierung nie aufhören soll.

E: Frage: Wie passt dein Konzept mit Paradigmen wie DevOps oder Contiuous Integration zusammen? Weil das was du machst ist für mich ein klassisches Wasserfallmodell.

I: Ist aber nicht ganz ein Wasserfallmodell, weil was wir hier haben ist mehr oder weniger ein Modernisierungsrad. Und dieses Modernisierungsrad muss nicht das gesamte Kernbanksystem betreffen, sondern kann einen eigenen Scope haben. Damit kann ich auch mehrere Modernisierungsräder parallel zueinander durchführen.

E: D.h. der Scope des Modernisierungsrades muss vorher immer definiert warden und sollte dem angepasst werden welche Zeithorizonte man sich setzt. Weil es gibt Modernisierungsvorhaben die sehr kurzfristig sind und welche die sehr langfristig sind. D.h. ein Rad wie bei George (Modernisierung von netbanking durch replacement) dürfte größer gewesen sein als beispielsweise eine Drei-Klick Kredit Komponente. D.h. der Inhalt der Modernisierung muss immer angepasst werden und dann ist das Folgerad (Folgemodernisierung) falsch. D.h. es gibt dann immer ein neues Rad mit einem anderen Scope und keinen Neustart des anderen Rads.

I: Du siehst das ein bisschen aus einer anderen Sicht als ich, und ich find das gut. Vor allem jedes Rad hat seinen eigenen Zeitplan und seine eigene Strategie. Vor allem die Räder können untereinander auch Dependencies haben.

E: Ja aber genau das ist der Mehrwert von so einem Konzept wie deinem, weil es dir erlaubt Dinge flexibel einzusetzen.

I: Genau, das ist auch der Sinn dahinter. Das Konzept wie beschrieben ist nur der Idealfall, kann aber nach belieben verändert werden, da es auch von den Rahmenbedingungen der jeweiligen Bank in Bezug auf Ressourcen, Geld und politischen Rahmenbedingungen abhängt. Im Großen und Ganzen ist das Konzept ein Top-Down Approach. Allerdings ist es sehr flexibel weil ich mir die Granularität aussuchen kann, ich kann mehrere Modernisierungsräder parallel auf einem Kernbanksystem ausführen, kann sie auch gruppieren und ich muss nicht unbedingt den BIAN befolgen. Z.B. FSSI wäre eine Alternative. Und auch im Bezug auf Projektmanagement kann ich ein anderes Vorgehensmodell verwenden. D.h. das Konzept an sich gibt nur den groben Prozessmechanismus vor und ist adaptierbar, deshalb ist es auch kein einzelner Prozess.

E: Vergiss den organisatorischen Scope nicht, weil das Business und die Technik müssen immer im Gleichschritt laufen, da vom Business das Geld kommt. Und vor allem wenn dann noch was ungeplantes in den Scope dazu kommt, müsstest du fähig sein im Rad einen Schritt zurück zu gehen, bzw das Rad entsprechend anzupassen (Stichwort Change Management).

I: Ein weiterer Vorteil ist Recurrency, da das Przesskonzept wiederkehrend ist.

E: Mir gefällt das nicht, stattdessen würde ich das nicht als altes Rad bezeichnen das wieder läuft sondern als neues Rad mit einem neuen Scope. Ich würde stattdessen die Wiederkehr weg nehmen.

I: Ok, aber die zeitliche Komponente ist sehr sehr langfristig im Bereich von 15 Jahren pro Durchlauf.

E: Ja ok, aber in deiner Diplomarbeit darf es nicht den Anschein haben dass du sofort nach einer Modernisierung wieder anfängst das Gleiche nochmal zu modernisieren.

I: Ich sag ja eigentlich man soll nie aufhören.

E: Ja aber das ergibt nicht immer Sinn und ist nicht im Sinne des Business. D.h. im Bezug auf das schnelle Drehen wie es hier angedeutet ist, würde ich vorsichtig sein.

I: Ja ich hab hier einen langen Scope so im Bereich 30-40 Jahren. … Ok, das Konzept ist vergleichsweise idealistisch da ich beispielsweise vorschlag 90% der Entwickler für Mehrwert im Tagesbusiness abzustellen und 10% nur auf Maintenance und Modernisierung.
E: Ist allerdings nicht realistisch, realistisch ist dass du von den 90% ein paar Prozent abzwackst und die für eine Technologieänderung einsetzt. Auf der anderen Seite ist das was du machst ein Prozesskonzept und damit eine Ebene über einem Prozess d.h. auf eine Metaebene. Und damit ist es ein valider Vorschlag. Da würd ich aber dann die Wertschöpfungs/Modernisierungsrate erhöhen auf 80% Wertschöpfung und 20% Maintenance und Modernisierung. Warum? Weil gewisse technologische Herausforderungen nur deshalb so schwierig sind, weil man sie nicht rechtzeitig umgestellt hat. D.h. man sollte einen bewussten Teil der Ressourcen einsetzen, um eine kontinuierliche technologische Verbesserung zu machen, unabhängig von der Businessseite. In der Realität ist das natürlich eher ein Problem. Das Konzept sollte aber genau das berücksichtigen weil es doch einen Mehrwert liefert.
I: Ok, das Konzept ist prozessgetrieben, wobei jeder einzelne Modernisierungsprozess über die Modernisierungsstrategie orchestriert wird, wobei sich auch unterschiedliche Modernisierungsstrategien festlegen lassen und die Performance über KPIs messen lässt. Darüber hinaus ist das Modernisierungsprozesskonzept in jedes Setup integrierbar.
E: Stimmt, es passt so gesehen überall, weil es agil ist. Die Frage ist nur wie schnell jedes Modernisierungsrad gedreht wird.
…
I: Ich hab auch bei den Nachteilen geschrieben, dass ein Projektmanagement im Prozesskonzept fehlt.
E: Ein Projektmanagement zu sowas wäre schon spannend, stimmt das wäre die nächste Arbeit. Vor allem wie koordiniert man sowas? Vor allem kann unter Umständen an den gleichen Services oder Funktionalitäten gearbeitet werden und dann muss man sich echt überlegen wie man mit sowas umgeht.
…
I: Und das Konzept beinhaltet auch einen PoC.
E: Ja, wobei das mit dem PoC würd ich noch ein bisschen ausbauen, sodass man auch die Learnings aus dem PoC verwendet. Ich würde das so machen, dass man zuerst den PoC und Learnings einholt und erst dann die Endplanung macht, weil man so gesehen zuerst mal ausprobiert was man sich überlegt hat und erst dann den großen Modernisierungsrollout startet.
I: Wobei man muss das nicht machen.
E: Naja wenn das Modernisierungsrad vom Scope her klein genug ist dann muss man das nicht machen aber wenns größer wird, dann wäre das schon geschickt.
…
I: (Beim durchgehen der Nachteile) Und der Prozess lässt viel Freiraum für falsche Entscheidungen.

E: Naja der PoC ist ein Sicherheitsmechanismus um falsche Entscheidungen zu vermeiden, bzw. deren Risiko zu verkleinern. Auch könnten nach jedem Prozessschritt Kontrollmechanismen in den Prozess eingebaut werden.

...

(Gesamtfeedback)

E: Good job! Gefällt mir. Bis auf die Punkte die mir so aufgefallen sind, gefällts mir. Das entspricht einem sehr schönen Metakonzept um genau das was zu tun ist, zu beschreiben. Daraus könnte man auch etwas entwickeln, wenn es jemand bezahlen würd. Vor allem du hast einen wichtigen Schritt gemacht, du hast eine Metaebene eingeführt die nicht im Doing verhaftet ist sondern eine Ebene darüber die Steuerung der Modernisierung übernimmt.

...

E: Die Frage ist für mich, wo ist hier die Grenze zwischen den Business Prozessen und den technischen Prozessen, das ist für mich noch nicht ganz schlüssig hier. Weil der BIAN ist ja eigentlich sehr nahe am Business Prozess. Er schlägt zwar Modularisierung vor für eine technische Architektur aber wo fängt dann konkret die technische Architektur an. Hier müsstest du eventuell nochmal etwas nachschärfen.

...

(Beim Durchgehen der eigentlichen Interviewfragen)

...

1. **Overall Questions about the process:**
   a. Did you understand the process?

      Ja.

   b. What is your overall opinion on the process?

      Für mich ist das ein wunderbarer Meta Ansatz um Modernisierungsprojekte zu steuern. Für jeden der Schritte die im Prozess angegeben sind, muss natürlich eine weitere Detaillierung stattfinden. Aber für mich ist der Prozess konsistent, wiederholbar und er macht aus der Sicht von Business und Technik Sinn. Und das auf Basis meiner Erfahrungswerte, sowohl aus der Businessebene als auch auf Implementierungsebene.

2. **Feasibility:**
   a. Do you think that this process is feasible to existing CBS?

      Absolut. Natürlich müsste man noch eine Ebene weiter gehen und die Prozesse darunter genauer definieren aber das Gesamtkonzept das hier vorgestellt wird macht absolut Sinn.

   b. If not, why?

3. Advantages / Shortfalls:

a. Where do you see room for improvements?

Für mich wäre wichtig Kontrollmechanismen im Konzept zu haben, weil alle diese Ansätze im Konzept, klingen sehr gut, müssen aber immer auf einen Realitätscheck stoßen, da sonst der gesamte Prozess sehr leicht in die Irre läuft.

b. Which preconditions should be met to make this process concept admissible?

Die richtige Metabene muss vorhanden sein. Also vor allem Geld und Ressourcen, aber das ist ja nicht das Thema hier. Eine Organisation die diesen Prozess verwenden möchte, muss die Bereitschaft zu Veränderung haben. Weil es darf keine Showstopper oder No-Gos geben, weil es immer so ist dass sich die Organisation und die IT Hand in Hand verändern müssen und es dort auch Wechselwirkungen gibt. Es kann nicht sein, dass das Business nur über die IT bestimmt und die IT nur der Befehlsempfänger ist, aber umgekehrt auch nicht, d.h. die IT darf nichts verhindern. Stattdessen muss es einen partnerschaftlichen Ansatz zwischen IT und Organisation geben um die Transformation der Geschäftsprozesse durchführen zu können.

c. Which strongpoints/shortfalls do you see with that process concept?

Eine Stärke ist definitiv die Flexibilität im Prozess und die flexible Nutzung des Prozesses, weil die Granularität und der Scope frei wählbar sind. D.h. man kann den Prozess für eine kleine Modernisierung aber auch für ein fünf Jahres Projekt anwenden. Der Vorteil ist auch, dass man diese verschiedenen Scopes auch parallel laufen lassen kann. Der Nachteil daran ist, dass durch die Offenheit und Flexibilität wiederum die Steuerung erschwert wird. Die funktionale Steuerung und die Governance auf allen Ebenen wird sicher eine Herausforderung für sich. Der Lösungsanatz für sowas ist natürlich nicht zu viel auf einmal zu machen. D.h. wenn jemand mit so einem Modernisierungsprozess los legt, dann muss er sich überschaubare Ziele setzen. Und überschaubar bedeutet nicht dass ich in fünf Jahren ein neues Kernbanksystem habe, sowas passiert einfach nicht, sondern dass ich in drei Monaten etwas habe das ich verwenden kann. Ein weiteres Risiko ist auch dass man den Detaillierungsgrad falsch wählt. D.h. dass man eine falsche Granularität oder zu viele Module für die Modernisierung wählt und damit nie zu einem Ende kommt.

d. What would you do different?

Guter Punkt. Ich hab natürlich grundsätzlich kein Problem mit einer Metaebene in Prozessen aber wenn man so etwas jemandem verkaufen soll, wird es schwierig werden wenn man die Prozesse unterhalb nicht komplett durchdefiniert. D.h. bevor das Prozesskonzept praktikabel und umsetzbar ist, muss auf jeden Fall die Ebene unterhalb genau spezifiziert werden. Das gesamte Konzept ist vielleicht etwas zu theoretisch für den praktischen Ansatz.

B.2. Interview 2

Interview between Alexander Gruber and the second expert on April 3rd, 2018.

I: Also als erstes schau ich mir das aktuelle Kernbanksystem an. D.h. ich schau mir an wo das Kernbanksystem modularisiert ist bzw. wo ich Modulgrenzen einziehen kann. Daraus soll im Weiteren eine funktionale Map generiert werden. Dadurch bekomm ich eine funktionale Topologie meines aktuellen Kernbanksystems das ich zu einer Baseline of Applications verarbeiten kann.

E: Ok. Wobei man kann sich das auch in Non-Functional Requirements ansehen (eher auf Business Ebene) und bei der Kapselung kann beispielsweise geschaut werden ob Shared Components (die von mehreren anderen Komponenten verwendet werden) abgrenzbar sind, also beispielsweise ob sie Multi Channel fähig sind. Z.B. Kunde oder gibt es nur ein Security Modul? Sind die Geschäftsprozesse Vertriebskanal unabhängig? Und vor allem sind hier auch schon Erfahrungen von anderen Kernbank Modernisierungen eingeflossen.

I: Verstehe. Als nächstes schau ich mir im Prozess die Bankorganisation an sich an. Jede Bank hat ihre Abteilungen die wiederum ihre eigenen Kernprozesse haben. Und jeder Kernprozess sollte im Kernbanksystem funktional abgebildet sein. Beispielsweise die Kreditabteilung braucht ihre Funktionalität um Kredite abzuwickeln und zu verwalten.

E: Ja, wobei hier diese Diskussion schon seit zwanzig Jahren geführt wird, d.h was passiert wo? Was passiert im Backoffice, was passiert im Frontoffice? Weil früher war es so, dass die Filiale an sich funktional relativ unabhängig war und vieles vom klassischen Backoffice mit gemacht hat. Und jetzt ist die Tendenz, dass alles ins Backoffice geworfen wird und alles zentral gemacht wird.

I: Ok, d.h. zuerst schau ich mir das aktuelle Kernbanksystem an und danach die Organisation der Bank.

E: Ja, wobei es hier mehr um die Schnittstellen geht.

I: Gut, sowie ich das dann hab schau ich mir die Zukunftsstrategie der Bank an, d.h. ich schau mir an welche Zukunftsstrategie der Bank ist, die ja dann auch funktional im Kernbanksystem abgebildet werden muss.

E: Ja, wobei im Moment Digital der Fokus ist. Alle Banken wollen zur 24h Bank werden und man versucht die bestehenden Prozesse so umzubauen, dass vom Kunden möglichst viel Online ohne Bankfiliale gemacht werden kann.

I: Ok, sowie ich die Baseline of Applications hab, sowie die aktuelle und die zukünftige Organisation der Bank kann ich weitergehen.

E: Ok, wobei man hier (bei der Baseline of Applications) nicht so sehr nach Abteilung gehen sollte sondern eher danach geht, Prozesse billiger zu machen. Es gibt seit zwanzig Jahren einen Trend viele Backoffice Funktionalitäten in nicht-Bank Betriebe auszulagern. Aber auch in der Bank direkt werden Kunde, Konto oder der Zahlungsverkehr in Töchter ausgelagert, die nicht dem Bankenkollektivvertrag unterliegen und dadurch billiger sind. D.h. man versucht nur das in der Bank zu behalten, was in der Bank bleiben muss.

I: Verstehe. Aus der Baseline of Applications und der Zielstruktur der Bank kann ich mir eine Liste aus funktionalen Gaps machen, die entweder zur Funktionalität des aktuellen Kernbanksystems hinzugefügt oder entfernt werden müssen. Und damit kann man dann eine Target Architecture erzeugen die dem BIAN konform ist. Wobei du hast hier mal gesagt dass es eine Alternative zum BIAN gibt?

E: Ja IBM hat mal vor fünfzehn Jahren etwas eigenes entwickelt und BIAN hab ich als Gesamtbankmodell noch nirgendwo eingesetzt gesehen.

I: BIAN unterteilt eine Bank de facto in Service domains, wobei die darunterliegende Ebene noch nicht wirklich ausspezifiziert ist.

E. Bei manchen Domains hab ich gesehen dass diese bereits relativ detailliert sind und bei anderen steht bis jetzt nur die Überschrift. Und das Zweite ist dass er sich bis jetzt nur auf einer allgemeinen Ebene befindet. Vor allem die Anforderungen an eine Bank werden immer mehr und insofern ist es noch nicht das überall passende Bankenmodell. Europa ist beispielsweise anders als die USA, dort gibt es kein Universalkonto, sondern eher Kreditkarten und da passt der BIAN nicht vom Geschäftsmodell her. Auch in Bezug auf Islamic Banking oder andere Spezifika wie Darlehen die in Österreich und Deutschland sehr stark vertreten sind aber in den BIAN noch keinen Eingang gefunden haben. Z.B. das Österreichische Sparen ist ein großes System auf das der BIAN nicht passt.

I: Also der BIAN ist nicht überall anwendbar.

E: Ja, so leicht ist der BIAN nicht anwendbar und auch unsere Bank passt so gesehen nicht in den BIAN rein, dafür ist es für unsere Bank kein Thema sich an den BIAN anzupassen. Ein Beispiel sind zum Beispiel Sicherheiten die nicht auf einen Kredit verknüpft werden sondern auf das Gesamtobligo des Kunden, um zu verhindern dass bestimmte Dinge mehrfach verpfändet werden.

I: Ok, wie gesagt der nächste Schritt ist, dass man eine Target Architektur erstellt.

E: Allerdings muss die Bank der Target Architektur zustimmen und es sollte vorher erhoben werden, wie BIAN konform die Prozesse der Bank sind und wo sind hier die Gaps. Vor allem das ist eine geschäftspolitische Entscheidung und die Bank muss hier auch dahinter stehen.

I: Was wäre die Alternative?

E: Naja die Alternative wäre, dass die Bank bei ihren Prozessen bleibt und einfach nur versucht zukunftsorientiert zu sein, eben wie im vorher genannten Beispiel der 24-Stunden Bank.

I: Ok, und die Target Architektur soll serviceorientiert sein und in Service Clusters eingeteilt sein und die Grundidee ist, dass man sich aus der BIAN landscape die Service Domain Clusters raussucht die man braucht, diese so anpasst wie man sie braucht, und danach technische Spezifikationen schreibt um von der jeweiligen aktuellen Komponente auf die BIAN konforme Zielkomponente zu kommen.

E: Beispielsweise die IBM hat hier einen anderen Weg vorgeschlagen, die unterteilen alles in Komponenten (SCS) und jetzt wird gerade diskutiert wie man zu diesen Komponenten kommt, siehe beispielsweise die Credit Suisse Studie die ich dir geschickt hab. Die Herausforderung hier ist, Grenzen zu finden anhand derer man ein Kernbanksystem in Komponenten unterteilen kann. D.h. wie muss ich die Komponenten schneiden, sodass sie nach außen hin möglichst unabhängig sind. Beispielsweise eine reine serviceorientierte Struktur ist nicht möglich weil es Geschäftsprozesse gibt, die dermaßen ineinander verwoben sind, dass man es schwer hat durch alle Services durchzuhaken. Aber man kann es stattdessen so machen dass man diese inneren Verwebungen lässt wie sie sind und nach außen hin Schnittstellen definiert die nicht so hochfrequent aufgerufen werden und damit leichter managebar sind.

I: D.h. man macht Baublöcke und versucht nicht alles zu zerteilen.

E: Ja wobei das alleine ist schon schwierig und braucht mitunter mehrere Anläufe. D.h. die Herausforderung ist beispielsweise 600 Applikationen auf 80 Komponenten zusammenzupacken. Wobei wie muss ich hier die Komponenten legen, sodass ich möglichst wenig Abhängigkeiten nach außen hab? Die Idee hinter diesen Komponenten ist dann, dass man sozusagen Testbeete für die Komponenten schafft um diese dann unabhängig voneinander in die Live Umgebung einsetzen zu können. Und hier ist SOA schon ein bisschen schief gegangen. Es wäre zwar schön wenns funktionieren würde, aber in der Praxis ist das so nicht umsetzbar.

I: Ok, gehen wir wieder zurück? Sowie ich die Target Architektur hab versioniere ich sie und hab meine BIAN konformen Blöcke. Danach muss ich mir überlegen wie ich jedes einzelne Modul konkret modernisiern kann. Jedoch nicht nur auf topologischer Ebene sondern auch auf technischer und Implementierungsebene. Summa Summarum hab ich dann ein Mapping von alter Funktionalität in einer alten Architektur auf neue Funktionalität in einer neuen Architektur.

E: Dann müssten die neuen Komponenten aber BIAN Komponenten sein.

I: Genau.

…

I: Wenn du die Möglichkeit hättest, wie würdest du einen Kernbanksystem Host modernisieren? Unter der Annahme dass du unbegrenzt Ressourcen hast.

E: Naja, die größte Herausforderung wäre dass man skilled Leute bekommt die das können. Und die Plattform muss stabil sein. Weil andere Plattformen sind nicht unbedingt so stabil wie am Host (z.B. Linux), und hier gibt es gerade bei den neueren Plattformen eine größere Fluktuation beim Personal. Das zweite das man sehen muss ist, dass es bei allen nicht-Host Plattformen alle fünf Jahre eine Trendwende gibt in Bezug auf die Technologie. Jetzt ist gerade im Clientbereich

AngularJS aktuell, in fünf Jahren wird das wiederum anders sein. Und allein der Erfahrung nach war in den letzten zehn Jahren, alle drei Jahre eine andere Technologie der Hit. D.h. wenn man einen Host modernisiert braucht man eine Programmiersprache von der man ausgehen kann dass sie die nächsten zwanzig Jahre hält, da ein Kernbanksystem doch zig Millionen Lines of Code beinhaltet.

I: Java wäre ein Kandidat und auch die Performance wäre mittlerweile gut genug.

E: Ja, wäre wohl ein Kandidat, allerdings muss man die Programme ganz anders schreiben, die müssen hoch parallelisierbar sein. Und man braucht eine financial library dazu, denn Java unterstützt nativ keine Finanzfunktionen. Dahingegen ist Cobol ja bis zu einem gewissen Grad für Finanzsysteme entwickelt worden und das bietet Java nicht.

I: In Cobol müsste es auch eine Library dafür geben oder?

E: Nein nein, Cobol wurde damals als kommerzielle Programmiersprache für wirtschaftliche Applikationen konzipiert. Beispielsweise wie Zahlen aufbewahrt werden oder Punktrechnungen gemacht werden, das ist alles für den Finanzsektor bzw. Rechnungslegung gemacht worden und hier muss man bei Java schon eher aufpassen. Beispielsweise wann wird eine Nachkommastelle abgeschnitten und wie wird genau gerundet? Das wird auch so von staatlichen Organen kontrolliert.

…

I: Ein Beispiel für ein Java basiertes Kernbanksystem wäre Infosys Finacle?

E: Ja, aber das wurde auch bereits Anfang der 2000er Jahre gemacht. Und generell, ob Mainframe oder nicht, es hängt immer davon ab wie etwas verarbeitet wird und auch ein Mainframe ist Java fähig. Allerdings ist auch hier das Risiko, dass man sich bei einer Modernisierung Richtung Java grundlegend vertut und ein neues Kernbanksystem nicht so zum Laufen bringt wie ein altes. Ich glaube generell dass ein Top-Down Approach kein guter Ansatz ist sondern wenn, dann eher umgekehrt da man sich im Großen und Ganzen leicht verschätzt.

I: Dazu komm ich noch, denn mein Modernisierungsprozess wie ich ihn hier darstell denkt über eine Zeitspanne von 10 Jahren bzw. mehr.

E: Ok, das ist was anderes, allerdings musst du hier auch sehen, dass die meisten Beraterfirmen sagen, dass ein Kernbanksystem durchschnittlich fünfzehn Jahre hält und danach muss man ein neues schreiben. Früher ist das ein bisschen abgefedert worden da das Business näher an der IT war und zuerst gefragt hat aber mittlerweile bekommt man eher die Vorgabe dass man ein neues Kernbanksystem schreiben soll.

I: Ok, zurück zum Thema. Sowie ich meine Target Architektur habe, muss ich jeder Komponente das zu modernisieren ist, ein Modernisierungsinstrument zuordnen. Dazu gehören beispielsweise Model Driven Development, der Code automatisch bzw. halbautomatisch in anderen Code unter einer anderen Architektur neuimplementiert. Dann gibt es noch Replacement, d.h. ich reimplementier dieselbe Funktion parallel zur alten neu, und setz sie dann anstatt der alten ein.

E: Dazu musst du aber voneinander unabhängige Module haben.

I: Genau. Eine Alternative wäre, dass man statt Reimplementierung etwas neues kauft, das anpasst und dann statt der alten Funktionalität in die IT Landschaft einsetzt, Zahlungsverkehr wäre dafür ein Beispiel. Das Nächste was es noch gäbe, wäre architektonisches Refactoring, d.h. ich bau beispielsweise Cobol Code wieder in Cobol Code um und das in mehreren Zyklen, falls benötigt. Oder wenn sich herausstellen sollte, dass eine Komponente gar nicht mehr gebraucht wird, weil sie nicht mehr in die Strategie passt dann kann man sich überlegen diese Komponente generell zu dekommissionieren. Sowie dann eine Entscheidung getroffen ist, welches Modul wie modernisiert wird, habe ich ein Mapping von Modul zu Modernisierungsinstrument.

E: Wobei du hier die Abhängigkeiten bedenken musst, sowie du Modul A modernisierst ziehst du Modul B mit. Vor allem ist es auch ein valider Ansatz dass eine Bank mehrere Kernbanksysteme hat, die sich gegenseitig Daten zuschicken und jeweils ihre eigene Datenhaltung haben. Und dann tut man sich allerdings mit so einem homogenen Ansatz eher schwer, vor allem weil alt und neu gleich sein muss.

I: Aber die Kernbanksysteme werden nicht alle das gleiche machen, d.h. deren Funktionen sind disjunkt oder.

E: Ja aber im Ziel bei dir muss das berücksichtigt werden, weil du willst alle drei Kernbanksysteme zu einem zusammenfügen. Und du darfst die Abhängigkeiten untereinander nicht vergessen.

...

I: Sowie ein Mapping zwischen Instrument und Modul besteht, mache ich mir eine Modernisierungsstrategie in der die Zeitdimension hinzugefügt wird und im Grunde genommen entschieden wird, welche Komponente wann und in welcher Form modernisiert wird. Danach ziehe ich einen Proof of Concept. D.h. ich nehme eine exemplarische Funktion und versuche sie in der gewählten Modernisierungsart zu modernisieren. D.h. ich schaue mal ob die Idee so überhaupt durchführbar ist. Die Learnings aus dem PoC kommen danach wiederum in die Modernisierungsstrategie um einen Realitätscheck in die Strategie einfließen zu lassen. Sowie das dann erledigt ist, baue ich den PoC sukzessive aus.

E: Ja, das ist vergleichbar mit einem Big Picture, in dem man sich anschaut womit man zu modernisieren anfängt. Ein Beispiel wäre die Modernisierung der Bar- und Unbarkomponente wobei Bar um einiges einfacher ist als die Unbarkomponente, da es sich hier im Prinzip nur um die Kassa handelt. Insofern ist das Risiko mit komplizierten Komponenten zu beginnen höher.

... Ich finde es aber dabei problematisch wenn man bei einer Modernisierung die Programmiersprache wechselt, da die Vernetzung dann doch eine andere ist. D.h. wenn das Altsystem stark vernetzt ist steigt auch das Risiko bei der Modernisierung.

I: D.h. es macht Sinn ein System zuerst zu transformieren um Abhängigkeiten untereinander zu reduzieren und erst danach die Programmiersprache in einem eigenen Modernisierungszyklus zu wechseln.

E: Generell ist davon abzuraten Kernbanksysteme mit einem Big Bang zu modernisieren. Bei manchen kleinen Banken mag das funktionieren, bei großen Banken ist das kein guter Ansatz.
I: Wurden bei euch auch PoCs gemacht? Bzw. habt ihr die neue Funktionalität gegen die alte regressionsgetestet?
E: Naja wir haben beispielsweise Buchungen parallel fahren lassen und dann geprüft ob die neue Buchungslogik dasselbe macht wie die alte. Und etwaige Differenzen sind dann näher betrachtet worden, sofern sie ungewollt waren.
...
I: Ok, Summa Summarum wird der PoC weiter ausgebaut, bis am Ende die implementierte Target Architecture heraus kommt. Dadurch wird idealerweise das Ziel zum IST-Stand. Und wenn das passt, dann kann man in weiterer Folge den nächsten Modernisierungszyklus angehen in einem beliebigen Zeitrahmen. Insgesamt ist der gesamte Ansatz ein Top Down approach.
E: Wobei du hier bedenken musst, dass die Bank immer wieder neue Anforderungen herein bekommt. D.h. die Target Architecture ändert sich ständig.
I: Ja, aber das rechne ich bereits in die Zielstruktur der Bank ein. Darüber hinaus kann man auch mehrere Modernisierungsräder parallel zueinander laufen lassen.
E: Ja, wenn die Räder untereinander entkoppelt sind und keine Abhängigkeiten untereinander haben. Das Problem ist halt, dass sie normalerweise nicht entkoppelt sind.
...
I: Im großen und Ganzen ist das vorgestellte Prozesskonzept eine konsistente Roadmap.
E: Ja, es ist mehr oder weniger ein Softwareentwicklungsmodell. Zumindest geht es in diese Richtung.
I: Und im Prozess argumentiere ich auch, dass Entwicklungsteams einen gewissen Prozentsatz ihrer Ressourcen für Modernisierung und Maintenance einsetzen sollen, da Modernisierung ein never ending Prozess ist.
E: Ja, das stimmt das wird bei uns seit 30 Jahren diskutiert. Bei uns gibt es Teams die einen Teil ihrer Zeit nicht in Kundenanfragen sondern in Maintenance stecken. Das wird auch von oben gefordert.
I: Aber keine 20% ihrer Zeit?
E: Kann mitunter schon vorkommen, hängt aber auch von den einzelnen Teams ab.
I: Ok und bei den Nachteilen hab ich geschrieben dass das Prozesskonzept doch auch ein wenig Highlevel ist.
E: Naja was das Prozesskonzept nicht löst ist die Monolithenauflösung, also wie man ein monolithisches Kernbanksystem in mehrere Komponenten schneidet.
I: Ok aber das ist auch nicht im Scope dieser Diplomarbeit, das würde deren Rahmen definitiv sprengen. Ok nun zum eigentlichen Fragebogen der Arbeit:

Interview Questions:

1. **Overall Questions about the process:**
   a. Did you understand the process?
      Ja.
   b. What is your overall opinion on the process?
      Ja es ist fast ein normaler Softwareentwicklungsprozess. Also dass ich zuerst das IST analysiere und danach das SOLL definiere ist eigentlich klar. Das Prozesskonzept ist ein Ansatz um Probleme zu lösen aber ob er wirklich am Software Engineering Boden hilft ist eine andere Frage. Es ist zumindest wichtig dass eine Rahmenstruktur gegeben ist.

2. **Feasibility:**
   a. Do you think that this process is feasible to existing CBS?
      Naja die meisten Banken stehen vor der Herausforderung dass sie zuerst ihr monolithisches Kernbanksystem in Komponenten schneiden müssen und da hilft das Prozesskonzept nichts. Aber wenn die Komponenten geschnitten sind, dann könnte er hilfreich sein. … Generell ist der Prozess ein Weiterentwicklungsprozess, und so gesehen ist er allgemein sicherlich anwendbar. Allerdings gibt es bei der Modernisierung von Kernbanksystemen Themen die generell angesprochen werden sollten, beispielsweise die Multi-Channel Fähigkeit von Komponenten. Z.B. gibt es Ideen dass sowohl der Mitarbeiter als auch der Kunde über die gleiche Software (in unterschiedlichen Channels) mit dem Kernbanksystem arbeiten.

   b. Do you think that this process is a starter for a long term modernization?
      Ja, wenn die Voraussetzungen dafür gegeben sind.

   c. If not, why?

3. **Advantages / Shortfalls:**
   a. What risks do you see with the proposed modernization process?
   b. What would you do different?
      Schau, das Problem ist wenn man so einen abstrakten Prozess hat der auf alles passt, dann passt das eh. Man kann nicht auf alle spezifischen Dinge einer Bank eingehen. Wenn man eine spezifische Bank hat, dann müsste man den Prozess zuerst anpassen. Weil jede Bank hat ihre eigenen Spezifika und so gesehen ist keine Bank wie die andere. Hier gibt es sicher viel zu berücksichtigen. Ein wichtiger Punkt ist halt wie ich nun wirklich das Target bzw. die Target

Architektur definiere und das in Abstimmung mit dem Business. Vor allem ist es bereits eine Kunst konsistente Requirements von der Bank als Kunden zu bekommen. D.h. Requirements die sich nicht ändern bzw. Requirements die für die IT brauchbar sind. Aber auf der Ebene wie du den Prozess beschrieben hast, passt er schon, allerdings geht er bei gewissen Themen nicht so in die Tiefe wie nötig.

c. What strengths do you see in this modernization process?

C. Exemplary Application Baseline Blueprint

The following blueprint is an exemplary baseline blueprint for the Day-End Processing of the CBS under modernization. It contains all subroutines as well as their type, implementation language, dependencies and interfaces to other modules.

Nr	Routine	Kind of Routine	Technology	Dependencies	Interfaces
1	Execute Standing Orders	Batchjob	RPG IV	Database - Accounts, Standing Order Tables	Core Banking DB, Function Calls
2	Cashless Settlement	Batchjob	RPG IV	Previous Routine - Account Current, Electronic Funds Transfer	Core Banking DB, Function Calls
3	Create Standing Order Protocol	Batchjob	RPG IV	Previous Routine, Standing Order Tables	Core Banking DB, Function Calls
4	Settle maturing capital savings accounts	Batchjob	RPG IV	Account Current, Account Tables (Inventory)	Core Banking DB, Function Calls
5	Process Compound Entries (Primanotas including Valutas)	Batchjob	RPG IV	Electronic Funds Transfer, Transaction Tables	Core Banking DB, Function Calls
6	Process Overdraft List	Batchjob	RPG IV	Previous Routine, Account Current, Account Tables (Giro)	Core Banking DB, Function Calls
7	Summarize Open Bookings for the Subledger	Batchjob	RPG IV	Account Current, Account Tables (Giro, Savings)	Core Banking DB, Function Calls
8	Prepare Subledger Processing	Batchjob	RPG IV	Previous Routine, Account Current, Account Tables (Giro, Savings)	Core Banking DB, Function Calls
9	Process Subledger Positions (Giro-, and Savings Accounts)	Batchjob	RPG IV	Previous Routine, Account Current, Account Tables (Giro, Savings)	Core Banking DB, Function Calls
10	Process General Ledger Positions (Inventory Accounts)	Batchjob	RPG IV	Previous Routine, Account Current, Account Tables (Inventory)	Core Banking DB, Function Calls

11	Perform direct ledger updates	Batchjob	RPG IV	Previous Routine, Account Current, Account Tables (Inventory)	Core Banking DB, Function Calls
12	Create Datacarrier Files	Batchjob	RPG IV	Electronic Funds Transfer, Account Current, Transaction Tables	Core Banking DB, Function Calls, File Export
13	Check for Remaining Open Entries	Batchjob	RPG IV	Account Current, Transaction Tables	Core Banking DB, Function Calls
14	Check for Balance Differences	Batchjob	RPG IV	Account Current, Account Tables (Inventory)	Core Banking DB, Function Calls
15	Test Suspense Accounts	Batchjob	RPG IV	Account Current, Account Tables (Inventory)	Core Banking DB, Function Calls
16	Prepare Interest Penalties	Batchjob	RPG IV	Account Current, Account Tables (Giro, Inventory), Transaction Tables	Core Banking DB, Function Calls
17	Create Protocol Interest Penalties	Batchjob	RPG IV	Previous Routine, Account Current, Transaction Tables	Core Banking DB, Function Calls
18	Create Error Report	Batchjob	RPG IV	Previous Routine	Core Banking DB, Function Calls
19	Create Report Overdrafted Accounts	Batchjob	RPG IV	Account Current, Account Tables (Giro)	Core Banking DB, Function Calls
20	Create Report Valuta Balance	Batchjob	RPG IV	Account Current, Account Tables (Giro)	Core Banking DB, Function Calls
21	Prepare Account Statements for Day-End Processing	Batchjob	RPG IV	Account Current, Account Tables (Giro, Savings)	Core Banking DB, Function Calls
22	Create Debit and Credit Sums for BMD	Batchjob	RPG IV	Account Current, Account Tables (Giro, Savings, Inventory)	Core Banking DB, Function Calls, Web Services
23	Create Credit Risk Reports	Batchjob	RPG IV	Account Current, Private-/ Corporate Loans, Account Tables (Giro)	Core Banking DB, Function Calls
24	Check internal temporary exemption of interests	Batchjob	RPG IV	Account Current, Private-/ Corporate Loans, Account Tables (Giro)	Core Banking DB, Function Calls
25	Create Status/Error Report	Batchjob	RPG IV	Previous Routine, Account Current	Core Banking DB, Function Calls
26	Create Overall Report	Batchjob	RPG IV	Previous Routine, Account Current	Core Banking DB, Function Calls

Table 3: Exemplary Application Baseline Blueprint

D. Mapping Legacy CBS Modules to the BIAN Service Landscape

The following Table contains the mapping of the legacy Core Banking Modules as outlined in chapter 4.5 against the service domain clusters as specified by the BIAN service landscape. The category below the bold module titles outline the name of the BIAN service cluster and the service domain in the right column name the service domain, containing the connected services.

Core Banking - Electronic Funds Transfer	
Payments	Payments Execution
Payments	Financial Gateway
Payments	Correspondent Bank
Payments	Cheque Processing
Core Banking - Account Current	
Product Management	Product Directory
Product Management	Discount Pricing
Product Management	Special Pricing Conditions
Account Management	Position Keeping
Account Management	Accounts Reveivable
Account Management	Account Reconciliation
Account Management	Position Management
Account Management	Fraud Detection
Account Management	Transaction Engine
Regulations & Compliance	Fraud/AML Resolution
Regulations & Compliance	Financial Accounting
Core Banking - Private- / Corporate Loans	
Loans& Deposits	Loan
Loans& Deposits	Leasing
Loans& Deposits	Current Account
Loans& Deposits	Deposit Account
Loans& Deposits	Consumer Loan
Loans& Deposits	Corporate Loan
Loans& Deposits	Corporate Deposits
Loans& Deposits	Corporate Lease
Loans& Deposits	Merchandising Loan
Loans& Deposits	Mortgage
Loans& Deposits	Fiduciary Agreement
Loans& Deposits	Savings Account
Collateral Administration	Collateral Allocation Management
Collateral Administration	Collateral Asset Management
Collateral Administration	Collections
Core Banking - Card Management	
Cards	Credit/Change Card
Cards	Card Authorization
Cards	Card Capture
Cards	Card Billing & Payments
Cards	Merchant Relations

Cards	Merchant Aquiring
Cards	Card Network Participant
Payments	Card Clearing
Payments	Card Financial Settlement
CRM - Customer Management / Customer Core Data	
Servicing	Card Case
Servicing	Customer Order
Servicing	Payment Order
Customer Management	Customer Relationship Management
Customer Management	Customer Agreement
Customer Management	Customer Access Entitlement
Customer Management	Customer Behavioral Insights
Customer Management	Account Recovery
Customer Management	Customer Event History
Customer Management	Customer Reference Data Management
Customer Management	Customer Precedents
Customer Management	Customer Proposition
Operational Services	Customer Billing
CRM - Customer Scoring / Account Management / Customer Risk Management	
Account Management	Position Keeping
Account Management	Cusomter Position
Customer Management	Customer Credit Rating
Account Management	Counterparty Risk
CRM - Document Management	
Document Management & Archive	Document Services
Document Management & Archive	Archive Service
Document Management & Archive	Correspondence
CRM - Customer Services	
Customer Services	Corporate Trust Services
Customer Services	Remittance
Customer Services	Currency Exchange
Customer Services	Bank Drafts & Traveller Checks
Customer Services	Brokered Product
Customer Services	Consumer Investments
Customer Services	Consumer Tax Handling
Customer Services	Consumer Advisory Services
Customer Services	Service Product
Corporate Financing & Advisory Services	Corporate Finance
Corporate Financing & Advisory Services	M&A Advisory

Corporate Financing & Advisory Services	Corporate Tax Advisory
Corporate Financing & Advisory Services	Public Offering
Corporate Financing & Advisory Services	Private Placement
Private Banking: Order & Portfolio Management / Risk Management	
Market Operations	Mutual Fund Administration
Market Operations	Hedge Fund Administration
Market Operations	Unit Trust Administration
Market Operations	Trade Confirmation Administration
Market Operations	Order Allocation
Market Operations	Settlement Obligation Management
Market Operations	Securities Delivery & Receipt Management
Market Operations	Securities Fails Processing
Market Operations	Trade/Price Reporting
Market Operations	Custody Administration
Market Operations	Corporate Events
Market Operations	Financial Instrument Valuation
Bank Portfolio & Treasury	Corporate Treasury Analysis
Bank Portfolio & Treasury	Corporate Treasury
Bank Portfolio & Treasury	Bank Portfolio Analysis
Bank Portfolio & Treasury	Bank Portfolio Administration
Bank Portfolio & Treasury	Stock Lending/Repos
Private Banking: Asset / Asset Liability Management	
Bank Portfolio & Treasury	Asset Securitization
Bank Portfolio & Treasury	Asset & Liability Management
Private Banking: Market Data Modeling / Market Risk Management	
Market Data	Invormation Provider Operation
Market Data	Marked Information Management
Market Data	Financial Market Analysis
Market Data	Financial Market Research
Market Data	Quant Model
Market Data	Marked Data Switch Administration
Market Data	Market Data Switch Operations
Market Data	Financial Instrument Reference Data Management
Market Data	Counterparty Administration
Market Data	Public Reference Data Management
Market Data	Location Data Management
Models	Market Risk Models
Models	Financial Inst. Valuation Models

Models	Gap Analysis
Models	Credit Risk Models
Models	Liquidity Risk Models
Models	Economic Capital
Models	Business Risk Models
Models	Customer Behavior Models
Models	Fraud Models
Models	Credit/Margin Management
Models	Production Risk Models
Models	Operational Risk Models
Models	Contribution Models
Private Banking: Trade & Investment	
Trade Banking	Letter of Credit
Trade Banking	Bank Guarantee
Trade Banking	Trade Finance
Trade Banking	Credit Management
Trade Banking	Credit Facility
Trade Banking	Project Finance
Trade Banking	Limis & Exposure Management
Trade Banking	Syndicated Loan
Trade Banking	Cash Management & Account Services
Trade Banking	Direct Debit Mandate
Trade Banking	Direct Debit Mandate
Trade Banking	Cheque Lock Box
Trade Banking	Factoring
Investment Management	Inv. Portfolio Planning
Investment Management	Inv. Portfolio Analysis
Investment Management	Inv. Portfolio Management
Investment Management	eTrading Workbench
Wholesale Trading	Trading Book Oversight
Wholesale Trading	Trading Models
Wholesale Trading	Dealer Workbench
Wholesale Trading	Quote Management
Wholesale Trading	Suitability Checking
Wholesale Trading	Credit Risk Operations
Wholesale Trading	Market Making
Wholesale Trading	ECM/DCM
Wholesale Trading	Program Trading
Wholesale Trading	Traded Position Management
Wholesale Trading	Marked Order
Wholesale Trading	Marked Order Execution

Table 4: Detailed Mapping of the Legacy CBS modules against the BIAN Service Landscape

Printed in Great Britain
by Amazon

78191337R00108